BATSFORD'S
Oxford
THEN AND NOW

BATSFORD'S
Oxford
THEN AND NOW

Vaughan Grylls

BATSFORD

PHOTO CREDITS
The publisher wishes to thank the following for kindly providing photographs for this book:

All "Then" photographs are courtesy of Oxfordshire County Council Photographic Archive,
except for the following:
Pages 12, 20, 30, 40, 42, 50, 54, 66, 74, 76, 84, 86, 88, 92, 94, 100, 116 and 122 courtesy
of Anova Image Library.
Pages 32, 82, 110 and 112 courtesy of English Heritage, National Monuments Records.

Thanks to Vaughan Grylls for taking all the "now" photography in this book.

Front and back covers show: Magdalen Bridge then (photo: Oxfordshire County Council
Photographic Archive) and today (photo: Vaughan Grylls).

AUTHOR'S ACKNOWLEDGEMENTS
On May morning, brave or foolhardy undergraduates have traditionally accepted any dare to
jump off Magdalen Bridge into the shallow River Cherwell. Accepting a commission to
photograph and write a book about Oxford bears some comparison, for there are dangers in
taking the plunge. There are those who have succeeded and there are those who have bruised
themselves in the shallows.

For me there were many who were experienced and kind enough to advise me where to jump.
Thus, where I have landed badly it is entirely my own fault.

In the space available here it is impossible to give credit to all those who have helped me.
What follows is, to my chagrin, unforgiveably attenuated.

My first and foremost acknowledgement is to my wife, Polly Powell, for suggesting this book.
Without her support it simply would not have happened. Those following were equally helpful in
various ways. My brother, David Grylls, Fellow of Kellogg College, Oxford, knew which way I
should go from the beginning, starting by locating an old press release about the Nuclear
Physics Laboratory. He went on to recommend Christopher Hibbert's excellent *Encyclopaedia of
Oxford*, as well as *Oxford: An Architectural Guide* by his colleague Geoffrey Tyack, to whom he
introduced me. Geoff is probably the world's leading authority on the architecture of the city and
it was therefore a great privilege to accept his generous offer to read my manuscript. The same
applies to Christopher Day whose knowledge of the history of Oxford is exceptional. My thanks
to both Geoff and Chris for their invaluable comments and suggestions. At the Oxford Local
History Archive in Westgate, Stephen Rench was knowledgeable and enthusiastic, bringing to
my attention the brilliant photographs of Henry Taunt and others, including images I would
certainly have overlooked without his guiding hand. At the Macdonald Randolph Hotel, Michael
Grange, General Manager, and John Escobar, Assistant Head Concierge, forgot for a moment
that they had a large hotel to run and took me patiently to one room after another in our joint
search for the exact place where Taunt took his photograph of St Giles' Fair over a century
before. At the Buttery Hotel in Broad Street, Felicity Wilson, General Manager, and Michael
Kapten did the same in locating the room where a photograph of Broad Street had been taken.
At the Sheldonian Theatre, my guide David Holt actually climbed scaffolding to take a
photograph for me and then introduced me to Richard Butcher from the building contractors
Beard and Co. Richard had us both clambering over the scaffolding (the Sheldonian was being
refurbished internally) to locate where Taunt had taken his wonderful shot, from a dizzying
height and with a huge plate camera, of the place where the 'Bridge of Sighs' would eventually
be built. Richard was also invaluable in describing, from a professional's point of view, how and
why the Sheldonian's extraordinarily designed ceiling had held up for over three hundred years.
That guided tour was a privilege. At Oriel College, Lady Morris, wife of the Provost, deserves
special thanks for rescuing me from my uninformed meanderings, providing instead a
thoroughly helpful guided tour of that splendid college. At Lincoln College, Stuart White, the
College Surveyor, and Jim Murden, Head Chef, were untiring. They literally opened doors that
had not been swung on their hinges for perhaps 50 years to help me get the images I needed
for this book. At Corpus Christi College, its President, Sir Tim Lankester, stood gamely with
undergraduate Grace Weaver where Thomas Case, one of Tim's Victorian predecessors, had
once stood. Grace took the trouble to wear subfusc for the shot. Afterwards I was offered tea in
the President's rooms, as well as more information about President Case. At every college the
porters I met were helpful and positive, not an easy task when their first responsibility is the
security of their college. I do hope they will not mind too much if I mention just one of them,
John Maguire of Queen's, to represent them all.

Last but certainly not least are Frank Hopkinson and David Salmo, my editors at Anova
Books. The suggestions and contributions they offered were invaluable and immensely
improved this book.

As you may imagine, it feels rather strange to find the place where another photographer
arrived long before you, noticed similar things, made comparable decisions and took that
defining shot. All this was given an extra twist for me when early one morning, quite by
accident, I captured my father's body-double, as a young man, walking across Magdalen Bridge.
My father had been at Oxford in the 1920s. He died in 1977. It is to his memory that I dedicate
Oxford Then and Now.

For my father, Herman
Who, long ago also cycled and strode o'er Magdalen Bridge
now and then

A Short History of Oxford

In the sixteenth century an unknown Oxford panegyrist asserted: 'If God himself on earth abode would make / He Oxford sure would for his dwelling take.' The city had come a long way from its beginnings seven hundred years before. The first building on the site was a modest church founded by Frideswide. Hiding on the banks of the Thames, she had escaped the attentions of a determined suitor, the Mercian King Algar. Blinded by lightning, he desisted and Frideswide set up a religious house for women. She eventually became patron saint for Oxford and its university.

What was to become Oxford was sited at the confluence of the Thames and the Cherwell. It was low-lying, marshy and damp, although for the Anglo-Saxons it had its attractions. They relied on rivers for transport and their cattle could be forded here. Surrounded by three rivers, it was easily defensible. It was also a good crossing place between the Anglo-Saxon kingdoms of Mercia to the north and Wessex to the south.

In the 890s the future City of Oxford was laid out. Aethelflaed is credited for this as she had an interest in both kingdoms, being a 'Lady of Mercia' and a daughter of King Alfred of Wessex. By c. 900, in the 'Burghal Hidage', we first see the new settlement specifically referred to as Oxnaforda and then again in 912 in the *Anglo-Saxon Chronicle*.

Oxford suffered its share of Danish raids and reprisals. In 1002 its Danish population was massacred. By 1050 Oxford's fortunes had risen and it ranked alongside Lincoln and Winchester as one of England's more important towns. However, in 1071 its fortunes fell again when many houses were demolished by the Norman Robert d'Oilly, to make way for his castle.

Oxford recovered and became a focus for the establishment of religious houses from the early twelfth century onwards and in 1155 received a charter from Henry II, granting its citizens the same privileges as those of London. Several Parliaments were held, including one in 1258, when the 'Provisions of Oxford' were promulgated as an attempt to limit the power of the King.

The University of Oxford can trace its beginnings to around 1117 when one Theobald of Etampes gave lectures in Oxford, followed by Robert Pullen who taught there between 1133 and 1138. In 1167 Henry II clashed with the King of France, who was harbouring Thomas Becket, the recalcitrant Archbishop of Canterbury. Henry ordered all English students at the University of Paris to return home. Many wisely decided to settle in Oxford – it was not far from London, it had a royal residence (useful for preferment), several religious houses with books (handwritten and thus expensive) and churchmen who could read and who, being at the edge of the Bishop of Lincoln's vast diocese, enjoyed significant freedom from the normal ecclesiastical interference of the period. In addition, Oxford had developed into a thriving commercial centre.

The earliest colleges were founded in the mid-thirteenth century and are, in alphabetical order, Balliol, Merton and University. Which came first depends on what you count – buildings, site, or endowment. The important point is that these colleges were established when Europeans were starting to translate the Greek philosophers and they were assisted by a relatively open-minded clergy who saw an opportunity of reconciling classical learning with theological orthodoxy. Clergy, teachers and students, being drawn from far and wide, found it efficient to converse in Latin. This made them appear foreign to the townspeople and fomented tensions between 'town and gown', culminating in the riot of 1355 in which more than 90 people perished.

The greatest struggles in Oxford's history were less to do with town and gown than with church and state. In 1370 the university finally escaped the Bishop of Lincoln's jurisdiction and in 1489 the Pope confirmed its independence from all ecclesiastical jurisdictions. In 1555 the Protestant 'Oxford Martyrs', Bishops Hugh Latimer and Nicholas Ridley, and Archbishop Thomas Cranmer, were tried for heresy in Queen Mary's reign. Latimer and Ridley were burnt at the stake on what is now Broad Street, followed by Cranmer in 1556. In 1559, within a year of Elizabeth's accession, all Catholic appointees at the university were ejected.

During the Civil War Charles I established his headquarters at Oxford in 1642, after the battles of Edge Hill and Turnham Green. Oxford surrendered in 1646 and from 1647 to 1649 many of the university's Heads of Houses were ejected. In 1650 Cromwell himself was elected Chancellor of the University. The Heads regained their positions on Charles II's accession in 1660. During the Great Plague of London (1665–66), Charles II moved the Court to Oxford.

In 1737 the city introduced a Licensing Act, banning the performance of plays, which were seen to attract the lazy and licentious. The university was not exempt from moral torpor. Edward Gibbon, author of *Decline and Fall of the Roman Empire* remarked that in his alma mater, Magdalen, 'indolence and greed had their unrestricted reign'. Similarly, when George III asked the lexicographer and poet Samuel Johnson for his opinion on the university, he replied that although 'he could not much commend their diligence', he thought the (University) Press was improving. The most outstanding achievements in Oxford during this century were artistic, entrepreneurial or both – the Radcliffe Camera (1737–49), the New Magdalen Bridge (1778), the connection of the Oxford Canal to the Midlands canal system (1790), James Sadler's balloon ascent (1784), the opening of Morrell's Brewery (1782) and the composition of Haydn's *Oxford Symphony* in 1788, which was dedicated to Oxford in 1791 when Haydn was awarded an honorary degree.

In the nineteenth century, the university regained its standing through the work of individuals such as Benjamin Jowett, Master of Balliol. Jowett's strenuous efforts to ensure that 'clever young men from poor homes' could attend the university were more than matched by the extensive re-building of the city and university throughout the Victorian period. Following the establishment of the Association for Promoting the Education of Women in Oxford in 1877, Elizabeth Wordsworth founded Lady Margaret Hall in 1878. Yet it would not be until 1974 that male colleges admitted women. By the century's end Great Britain was running the world's largest empire, and Oxford ensured that its future leaders were recruited and taught appropriately. Candidates were also drawn from the colonies and in 1875 the Indian Institute was founded.

In the nineteenth century, religious controversy returned. With some success, the Oxford Movement attempted to move the Church of England back to its Roman roots. But the Martyrs' Memorial was erected in St Giles', providing permanent embarrassment for the Movement's devotees. A much more resonant argument was sparked in 1860 by an extraordinary debate in Oxford over Charles Darwin's *On the Origin of Species*. That debate was a milestone in modernity.

Two other nineteenth-century initiatives made an impact far beyond Oxford. The first was the Oxford University Press, which became the world's largest university publishing house. Its fortunes were built on the *King James Bible* and the *Oxford English Dictionary*. These were exported in vast numbers throughout the English-speaking world and beyond, defining the culture and language of the country more extensively than any other works. The second was the founding of Morris Garages in 1898. From this beginning, William Morris introduced popular motoring to Britain and its empire. The economy and society of Oxford underwent a transformation after 1922, as reasonably priced and reliable cars began to be mass-produced in Cowley. In 1959 the Morris Mini was launched and by the early 1970s more than 20,000 people worked at the Morris Motors and Pressed Steel Fisher plants. Morris (later Lord Nuffield) founded Nuffield College in 1937. Sadly, his company closed after a long decline, but Minis are made again in Oxford, now by BMW.

Penicillin, one of the greatest life-savers of the twentieth century, was first used at the Radcliffe Infirmary in 1941 and other significant medical advances have been associated with the city. A record was set in 1954 by a 25-year-old medical student, Roger Bannister, who ran the first four-minute mile at the Iffley Road running track.

Throughout the twentieth century the people of Oxford have addressed ethical issues fearlessly. In 1914 the President of Corpus Christi announced that if any of his staff or students joined the armed forces they would not be welcome back at his college. In 1933 the Oxford Union voted against fighting for King and Country. In 1942 at the height of war, Oxfam was founded in the city. Throughout the 1950s there were frequent 'ban the bomb' demonstrations and in the 1960s and 1970s several rallies against the Vietnam war.

In various ways Oxford has diversified. Its new university, Oxford Brookes, at Headington, was given a charter in 1991 but can trace its origins back to the founding of the Oxford School of Art in 1865. It has been named the UK's leading modern university by the *Sunday Times* eight times between 1998 and 2008. By 2005, 27 per cent of the population of Oxford were from ethnic minority groups. Oxford has always been cosmopolitan and today is one of the most diverse smaller cities in the UK.

From Lewis Carroll to Philip Pullman, many Oxford authors have used the city as a backdrop or inspiration in their writings. A wider television audience was reached in 1981 with the acclaimed adaptation of Evelyn Waugh's *Brideshead Revisited*, later followed by Oxford-based programmes such as *Inspector Morse* and *Midsomer Murders*.

Oxford can at times present challenges and irritations – its transport system, for example, is a perennial source of conflict. But the city's drawbacks are more than made up for by the wonder of its history, traditions and beauty. Whether or not God would still like to dwell in Oxford, it bears comparison with Prague, Venice or Florence – or indeed with any city on earth.

Introduction

This book uses photographs to show Oxford as it was and Oxford as it is today. Yet it is not simply past and present that are contrasted. Oxford is a busy commercial city into which a university was inserted, cuckoo-like, over 800 years ago. The contrast between city and college, marketplace and cloisters, still persists.

For me, much of Oxford University's architecture appeared at first sight to have remained unchanged for a century or more. However, when I looked at old photographs I was surprised to see that extensive changes had often been designed to appear as though nothing had happened. Nearly every stone building has been re-faced. Whole new buildings have been erected, looking as though they have been there for ever. Oriel College's Rhodes Building on the High Street and Hertford College's 'Bridge of Sighs' are each less than a century old. Yet they have blended in with the architecture and, in the case of the second, become instant history.

Of course, modern academic structures have also been built in Oxford. Some have matured well, such as the Sir Thomas White building at St John's College. But the Dyson Perrin Laboratories have fared appallingly, as these photographs show. As for the Said Business School, it is perhaps too early to say.

Apart from completely new colleges, however, obviously modern buildings have remained the exception. Why was the appearance of permanence, of the unchanging, so important? Why was it so artfully maintained? Was it simply a fondness for traditional architecture? Surely not – there must be something more. Would it be too fanciful to suggest that these convincing displays of permanence, these visual celebrations of the eternal, were subconsciously welcomed as anchors and comforts by Oxford academics whose research and learning have restlessly challenged accepted truths and reshaped the contours of thought?

But Oxford is also a city of commerce as well as a university city and here market forces continually threaten stability of appearance. In Cornmarket Street, Woolworths has moved twice in 70 years, in both cases directly across the road, demolishing historic buildings in its path. Now it no longer enjoys a presence and its former buildings have been colonised by other high-street chains.

Change is not confined to buildings. For the visitor, Oxford's greatest scourge is the relentless procession of buses operated by competing companies. St Giles' and Carfax are currently *de facto* bus stations. In the case of several of the 'now' photographs, I had to take them in the split second between the disappearance of one bus and the arrival of another. But what the camera cannot elude are the garish yellow road markings, the traffic lights, the massive direction signs. The recent addition of 'pedestrian zones' has completed the visual cacophony. Neo-Victorian rubbish bins, lamp standards and bollards are set in contrasting styles of paving, thus giving little opportunity for the eye to rest. Luckily, historic Brasenose Lane has so far escaped these upgrades.

Perhaps I am being too hard on the 'now' in Oxford. We cannot know what these streets once smelled like. What we do know is that the sulphurous fumes of thousands of coal fires, factory chimneys and gas-lamps rotted the soft stone of Oxford's medieval buildings more effectively than sugar rots teeth. What such fumes did to the people in the Victorian photographs we can only imagine. They evidently bustled about energetically: in the main streets, Victorian Oxford looks busy. Yet in other pictures there are very few people, making them look suspiciously posed. On Broad Street, a hansom with its cabbie is drawn up outside Balliol. On Turl Street a family group waits patiently outside Lincoln. Exposures were long and people had to stay still to be properly captured. That and the need to make an outdoor scene picturesque by adding a few people here and there – a convention inherited from painting – renders these particular photographs charming. Today's camera lenses make objects closer to the camera appear larger; an obvious point to make you would have thought, until you glance at some of the 'then' images, such as this one of the High Street (opposite). In this image the adults between the camera lens and the shop awnings appear roughly the same size. This photograph and many others reproduced in this book were taken by the gifted Oxford photographer Henry Taunt (1842–1922). Apart from his aesthetic eye and evident technical ability, he deserves credit for taking certain pictures at all with a heavy, cumbersome plate camera. His shot from the top of the Sheldonian Theatre to where the 'Bridge of Sighs' would eventually arise is a most impressive achievement.

Many Oxford buildings have maintained their shell but been adapted to new uses. Oxford's once notorious prison is now a luxury hotel. William Morris's grandest car showroom is now Oxford Crown Court. Yet Blackwell's Bookshop has worked hard to appear to have changed as little as possible. The famous shop has deliberately hidden its light under a bushel by expanding hugely – to the amazement of visitors – into an enormous underground room.

For all its faults and irritations, Oxford, more than any other university city loves to take you (the visitor) by surprise. It revels in hiding and revealing. You can wander into a forbidding prison and find yourself in a welcoming hotel, or step from a noisy street through a college gate into the timeless peace of an ancient quadrangle ... only to discover more quadrangles, and yet more beyond. Was it this element of surprise that inspired Oxford writers such as Lewis Carroll or C.S. Lewis or, more recently, Philip Pullman, to offer their readers a rabbit hole, a looking-glass, the back of a wardrobe or a hole cut in space as secret passages to a parallel world?

Vaughan Grylls

VIEW OF THE
OXFORD SKYLINE

As seen from Elsfield

Elsfield, a village overlooking the Thames Valley a few miles north of Oxford, provides one of the best panoramas of the city. It is the classic view of Oxford's dreaming spires, as seen in this photograph taken in May 1969. Many of Oxford's iconic buildings are readily identifiable. Most prominent is the dome of the Radcliffe Camera (1737–48), to its left the spire of St Mary's (early fourteenth century) and, to its right, the spire of All Saints (rebuilt 1718–20). St Mary's was used for Oxford University's main ceremonies until the building of the Sheldonian Theatre in 1669. In 1971 All Saints was declared redundant, because of its falling congregation, becoming the library of Lincoln College in 1975.

Forty years on, the view is virtually unchanged. The outline of Merton College Chapel tower (circa 1450) at the extreme left can be seen clearly, backlit by a late afternoon autumn sun. In this direction, Oxford's green belt has been largely preserved. But not far to its left the John Radcliffe Hospital (see inset) has been developed significantly between 1973 and 1979. The hospital was extended again in 2007 following the closure of Radcliffe Infirmary in the city centre. John Radcliffe Hospital's footprint is now as large as the whole of Oxford's ancient city centre. Many of Oxford University's medical departments are to be found here, including the world-famous Nuffield Institute for Medical Research. What cannot be seen, but can be heard, is the sound of traffic from the ring road lying between Elsfield and Oxford. Oxford, although a city famous for education and dreaming spires, originated as the place where the Thames could most easily be forded by early medieval travellers, journeying between the Midlands and the South or London and Wales. Oxford's location remains as important now as then.

THE RADCLIFFE CAMERA

An Oxford landmark

This Oxford landmark was designed by the architect James Gibbs as a domed library. It was built between 1737 and 1748 and takes its name from a bequest of £40,000 by the physician John Radcliffe, a Fellow of Lincoln College. It has been known as the Radcliffe Camera (after the Latin for room) since 1862. Nicholas Hawksmoor was the first choice for architect but he died before work could start. Gibbs was offered the commission and proposed to design a rectilinear library. The fund's trustees said he could design what he liked provided it was as round as Hawksmoor had intended. After all, Hawksmoor had proposed the layout of the square in which it would stand. Gibbs accepted but took the trustees at their word and designed something that utterly ignored the austere classical Palladianism that was then so popular in England. Yet it was a masterpiece, which could have honoured baroque Rome. This photograph was taken in 1865, when the newly dubbed Camera was little more than a century old. Already, it is suffering from the ravages of soot.

Gibbs' building stands unchanged, its recently cleaned and refaced stonework gleaming in the early morning sun. Also unchanged is the main Bodleian Library, a tower of which can be seen behind, as well as Radcliffe Square paved with large pebbles rammed into gravel, as first specified in 1771. The Radcliffe Camera became part of the Bodleian Library in 1861 and holds books from the English, History and Theology collections. The square in which it stands is often referred to as 'the heart of Oxford'. Buried beneath this quiet scene are the busy, labyrinthine vaults of one of the largest libraries in the world.

THE MARTYRS' MEMORIAL

Designed by George Gilbert Scott in 1841–42

This magnificent monument, seen here in 1899, was built by George Gilbert Scott between 1841 and 1842. Scott based his design on a late thirteenth-century cross at Waltham Cross in Hertfordshire, one of those erected by Edward I in memory of Queen Eleanor. The Martyrs' Memorial commemorates three prelates, Archbishop Thomas Cranmer, Bishop Hugh Latimer and Bishop Nicholas Ridley, who were burned at the stake in 1555 (Latimer and Ridley) and 1556 (Cranmer) at Oxford for their Protestantism. Two of the statues by the sculptor Henry Weekes can be seen on the second tier, Latimer to the left and Ridley to the right. Cranmer's statue faces north. The monument was built as something of a Protestant riposte to the Anglo-Catholic Oxford Movement, then in its ascendancy.

The coats of arms on the memorial have been painted in recent years. Its railings have disappeared and the mass of ivy on St John's College has been replaced by a non-evergreen creeper. St Giles', where the memorial is located, is now one of the most congested areas in Oxford. However, when the memorial was built this spot offered more space for contemplation than Broad Street, where the martyrdoms actually took place.

THE ASHMOLEAN MUSEUM

The first university museum in the world

The museum was founded by Elias Ashmole in 1686 with a collection of curios he inherited from the will of the famous gardener John Tradescant of Lambeth. It would become the first university museum in the world. In 1885, when this photograph was taken, this building (the previous one still stands in Broad Street) was only 40 years old. The university wanted something in the 'Grecian' style and so appointed Charles Robert Cockerell, then the country's leading architect in classical forms. It would be the last major, classically styled building in Oxford before Victorian Gothic became fashionable. Cockerell's building uses a mix of classical styles, an approach that reflected the museum's superb, if eclectic, collection. Highlights include the Alfred Jewel, an Anglo-Saxon gem with the inscription 'Alfred ordered me to be made', an extensive collection of Italian Renaissance paintings and drawings, and Guy Fawkes's lantern.

The corner from which this photograph was taken is the busiest traffic junction in Oxford. On 31 December 1999 a painting by Cézanne was stolen from the Ashmolean. The Sackler Library, with a collection focusing on archaeology, art history and ancient history, opened here in 2001. Funded by Dr Mortimer Sackler, the library contains works formerly held by the old Ashmolean Library, the Classics Lending Library, the Eastern Art Library and the History of Art Library.

THE RANDOLPH HOTEL

Oxford's first luxury hotel

Left: Constructed in 1863–66 by William Wilkinson in a simplified Victorian Gothic style, the Randolph was the first modern, luxury hotel in the city. It was built to accommodate the new railway age. Staying at the Randolph became *de rigueur* for any visitor of any importance, a role the hotel has maintained. Every American president who has stayed in Oxford has used the Randolph. It was from here that an early guest, Henry James, wrote about his characters in *A Passionate Pilgrim* (1871) visiting the university's colleges. When the book was published, visitors, especially Americans, flocked to the hotel. In this photograph of 1890, a coach and four is drawn up before the entrance with its newly erected iron porch.

Above: The lamp-standards have changed, the signs either side of the entrance have been replaced, small extensions to the pillars above the roundels have been made, and the vestibules flanking the entrance have been brought forward. Other than these small changes, the exterior remains the same. If anything, it is cleaner. Looking back at the 1890 photo the stonework already appears encrusted with soot: it was taken 66 years before the Clean Air Act was introduced. Major refurbishments have taken place since the Randolph was first built, the last being in 2000. The hotel is now known formally as the Macdonald Randolph after it was acquired by the luxury hotel chain of that name. Inside, there is the Morse Bar, named in recognition of the Oxford-based television drama *Inspector Morse*, whose cast stayed at the hotel in 2005.

ST GILES' FAIR

An annual fair that dates back to 1624

Starting as the St Giles' Parish Wake in 1624, it later became known as the St Giles' Feast. In the 1780s it was a toy fair and by the early 1800s it was a general fair for children. By the 1830s the fair had expanded beyond children's entertainment to include goods for sale, as well as booths and sideshows for adults. With huge crowds in the late nineteenth century there were attempts to suppress the fair on the grounds that it encouraged rowdy and licentious behaviour. These were unsuccessful and the St Giles' Fair has continued to be held more or less ever since on the Monday and Tuesday following St Giles' Day (1 September). This photograph was taken in 1906 from a room at the Randolph Hotel. Ivy completely envelops St John's College to the right.

The room from which the 1906 photograph was taken is now called The Presidential Suite. Oxford alumnus Bill Clinton has stayed there several times. The building with the pediment next door has been built since 1906 and at least one more building has been added to the one on its left. As Oxford undergraduates are usually away on vacation during the St Giles' Fair, the annual celebration is enjoyed by Oxfordshire locals and is an occasion of 'town before gown'.

THE LAMB AND FLAG

Owned by St John's College since 1695

Left: There cannot be many academic institutions that have owned a pub for as long as St John's College. They have owned theirs since 1695. Parts of the original building, photographed here in the mid 1970s, can still be seen in the pub. Judging from the passage below the sign, it once served as a coaching inn. The Lamb and Flag takes its name from the two symbols of St John the Baptist, the saint for whom the college is named. There have been several famous drinkers here, including Thomas Hardy, who may have written some of *Jude the Obscure* here, and The Inklings, a literary club that included C.S. Lewis and J.R.R. Tolkien.

Above: At first glance, little seems to have changed in more than 30 years. The Lamb and Flag has lost its Watney's designation as well as its sandwich-only menu. Today, like all Oxford pubs, a board outside boasts a restaurant-quality menu. This upgrade may have something to do with the fact that in 1997, St John's College took back the lease of the pub. Since then the college bursar has been the titular licensee. St John's College now offers Lamb and Flag postgraduate studentships funded partly by the profits from the pub. The Lamb and Flag has been used in the Oxford-based television series *Inspector Morse*.

ST JOHN'S COLLEGE, FRONT QUAD

Alumni include former Prime Minister Tony Blair

St John's Front Quad takes the evolved form of the classic Oxford quadrangle, which was first employed at Mob Quad, Merton College, in 1304. Here the architecture is monastically influenced, with arches that lead to staircases and with students' rooms reached from the top of each staircase. This quad was built as St Bernard's College between 1437 and the 1470s. In 1539 St Bernard's was dissolved and then re-founded in 1555 by Sir Thomas White and the Merchant Taylors Company. It became one of the richest colleges in Oxford. St John's took its name from the patron saint of tailors, St John the Baptist. This photograph was taken in May 1967.

The gatehouse and parapets have been completely refaced with stone that is harder-wearing than the soft, local, traditional varieties – Headington and Taynton freestone. This process of gradual replacement has been taking place all over Oxford for many years. Nothing else has changed in the Front Quad, ignoring for a moment the un-posed figures and the un-picturesque modern barrow. In many professions St John's can claim famous alumni: in poetry alone, Robert Graves, A.E. Housman and Philip Larkin. In politics, a famous graduate is former Prime Minister Tony Blair.

ST JOHN'S COLLEGE, SIR THOMAS WHITE BUILDING

A modernist addition to St John's fifteenth-century architecture

Left: To increase its undergraduate accommodation, St John's College commissioned architect Sir Philip Dowson of Arups to design a range of study/bedrooms to be built within its ancient precincts. It was a bold stroke and starting in 1970 it took five years to complete. It was named after St John's founder Sir Thomas White. The building's main feature is its brutal bush-hammered concrete, which was fashionable in the late 1960s and early 1970s. But this is softened slightly by turrets clad in French limestone.

Right: In 1976 the Sir Thomas White Building won a Concrete Society Award and, more than 30 years later, it looks better than it did originally – which is more than can be said for many modernist buildings. Foliage and shrubbery cleverly grown close to the college has made it appear more attractive over the years.

WORCESTER COLLEGE

A small part of Gloucester remains in Worcester

Worcester College was founded in 1714 with a modest bequest from a baronet of that county. If Worcester College had not run out of money by the 1720s, its cottage-style buildings on the south range of its main quad (shown right) might not have survived. These buildings belonged to Gloucester College (originally Gloucester Hall), Worcester's forerunner, and the plan was to sweep them away as they would detract from the intended classical splendour of the newly endowed college. An example of the new college is the 1720 library, which can partly be seen on the left. The south range was built in the fifteenth century as monastic offices, or *camerae*, and over each door is a carved shield of arms of the monastery associated with Gloucester College. In this photograph from 1870 two men stand outside one of these 'cottages'. The grounds were laid out in 1823 by the college's bursar Richard Gresswell.

With the start of the Victorian era and the enthusiasm for the medieval over the classical, the south range at Worcester survived. This photograph shows how astonishingly unaltered Worcester's 'cottages' have remained. Famous alumni of Worcester include the author Thomas de Quincey, media mogul Rupert Murdoch and the senior drama critic of *The New Yorker*, John Lahr.

SOMERVILLE COLLEGE

One of the first women's colleges to be founded at Oxford

Left: In this photograph from 1904 a group of young women in theatrical costume pose before the entrance to the new library of what was once called Somerville Hall, founded in 1879. These Somerville students are most likely dressed for *Demeter, a Mask*, specially composed for them in 1904 by the poet Robert Bridges. The hall was renamed Somerville College in 1894. Somerville's famous alumni include writer and pacifist Vera Brittain, Indian Prime Minister Indira Gandhi, politician Shirley Williams, authors Iris Murdoch and Dorothy L. Sayers, and British Prime Minister Margaret Thatcher.

Above: As a women's college originally, Somerville's undergraduates soon attracted the pejorative term 'blue-stocking' from the university's men. This was in recollection of the society of the same name set up in the eighteenth century by a group of women of intellect who preferred to discuss ideas rather than forever be confined to a life of trivia and ornament. In this photograph a member of the college walks past the entrance to the library at the exact place where her predecessors dressed in Ancient Greek clothes over a century earlier.

BROAD STREET

Showing Balliol College, Trinity College and the Sheldonian Theatre

Left: The Protestant martyrs Cranmer, Latimer and Ridley were burnt at the stake here, although their monument is in St Giles' (see page 12). Clearly there was an important hansom cab rank in the middle of 'The Broad'. On the left is Balliol College, followed by the grand entrance to Trinity College and, further along, the awning of Blackwell's Bookshop. To the right of the old houses, in the far distance, is the Clarendon building, the Sheldonian (with its so-called emperors' heads) and Exeter College. This photograph, with two men pushing a handcart on the left, a man in a boater swinging his cane and a student in a mortar-board on the right, encapsulates 'town and gown' circa 1880.

Above: A large tree obscures the entrance to Trinity College and the bulk of the New Bodleian Library rises on the horizon. The old houses at the end were replaced by the Indian Institute in 1882–84 – now the university's Faculty of History Library. Exeter College is scaffolded and the building next to it has replaced the one in the 'then' photograph. Interestingly, it has been built to exactly the same proportions. The taxi rank has gone and vans now dominate as the city allows temporary parking here for deliveries and collections. This image was taken from what was once Henry Taunt's photographic premises. A brilliant photographer, he is responsible for the majority of the nineteenth- and early twentieth-century images in this book.

BALLIOL COLLEGE

Perhaps the oldest college in Oxford

The traditional date of Balliol's foundation is 1263, although there is no hard evidence for such precision. However, if its age is to be taken from the date when its members first lived communally on its present site, then Balliol is the oldest college in the university. The recently completed Broad Street facade of Balliol College is shown here with a hansom cab drawn up before it. Built in 1867–68, it was designed by the Manchester-based architect Alfred Waterhouse. The rich donor who funded the building believed he was a descendant of the founder of the college, John de Balliol. One assumes Balliol's Master and Fellows thought it wise not to question him further. At this time many undergraduates were rich enough to hire hansom cabs as a matter of course.

Alfred Waterhouse's building remains in good condition, other than some wear and tear on the stone coping. Bicycles came into popularity in the late nineteenth century, assisted by the huge interest in the University Bicycle Club's annual race against Cambridge. There are now more than 150,000 bicycles in use in Oxford and more than 3,000 are stolen every year. Balliol receives more applications than any other college in Oxford. This is unsurprising, as the number of former students who have become leaders in their fields is most impressive. In politics alone its alumni include the pioneer of political economy Adam Smith, three Prime Ministers – Herbert Asquith, Harold Macmillan and Edward Heath – and the Mayor of London, Boris Johnson.

Trinity College was founded in 1555, although it can trace its beginnings through its predecessor Durham College to 1291. Shown here is the Jackson Building in the Front Quad soon after it was completed in 1885. Designed by Sir Thomas Jackson in the style of a Jacobean country house, it included 27 sets of rooms for undergraduates, a Junior Common Room, a lecture room and a room for the dean.

TRINITY COLLEGE

Showing the 1885 Jackson Building

This now-mellowed neo-Jacobean building overlooking its peaceful park-like
quad is a mere step away from the bustle of Broad Street. On the right can be
seen the cupola of Sir Christopher Wren's Sheldonian Theatre. Famous Trinity
alumni include English Civil War general Henry Ireton, Prime Minister William Pitt,
playwright Terence Rattigan and former editor of *The Times* Peter Stothard.

BLACKWELL'S BOOKSHOP

Owned by the Blackwell family since 1879

Left: Blackwell's was founded in 1879 by Benjamin Blackwell (son of Oxford's first city librarian) at 50 Broad Street, selling academic books from just one room. The classical front of Blackwell's hides typical timber-framed structures still being built in Oxford in the eighteenth century. This was at a time when brick and stone was more commonly used in English building. That is not the only thing hidden, for underneath Blackwell's and stretching under Trinity College next door, is the largest underground bookstore in the world. The Norrington Room, as it is called, was opened in 1966. This photograph was taken at the time of the completion of this amazing and unseen engineering work.

Above: Blackwell's is still family owned and now has more than 60 retail outlets across the UK. This original building appears, at first glance, completely unchanged. Yet look again at the store windows. Although the awnings are out and they are therefore in shade, the windows have been re-glazed, but with eighteenth-century-style bars to give the shop front a suitably aged appearance.

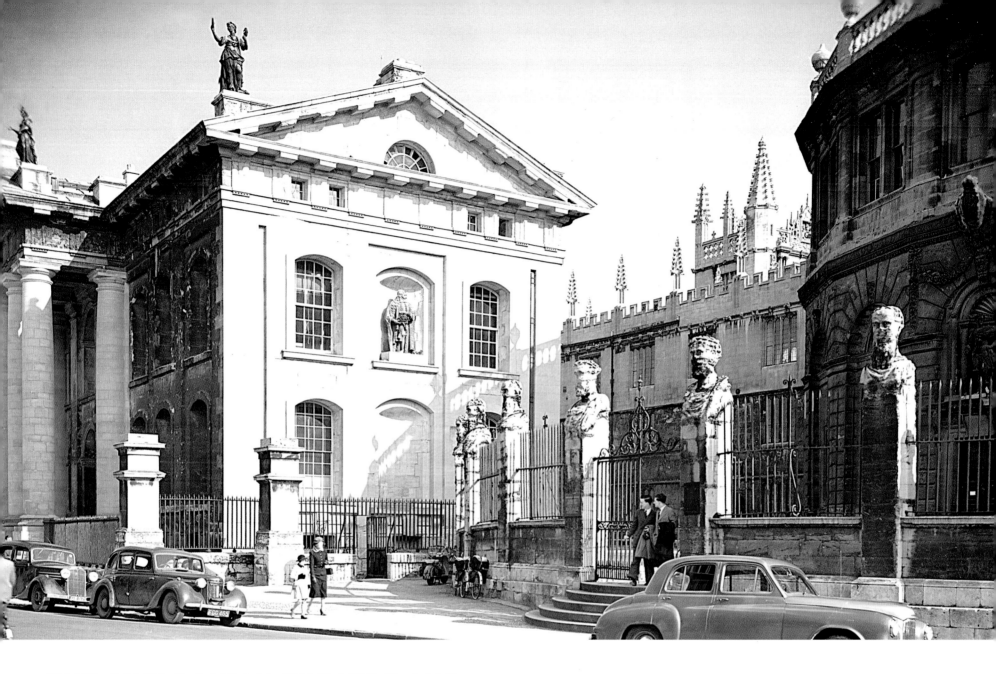

THE SHELDONIAN THEATRE AND
THE CLARENDON BUILDING

Designed by Christopher Wren and Nicholas Hawksmoor

The Sheldonian Theatre, to the right, was designed by Christopher Wren and built in 1664–67 as a new hall for university ceremonies, such as graduations and public performances. Its name comes from its benefactor Archbishop Gilbert Sheldon, while 'theatre' refers to Wren's inspiration, the second-century-BC Theatre of Marcellus in Rome. This was the first major commission for the future architect of St Paul's in London and the first in Oxford to be inspired so directly by classical antiquity. At that time, Wren was Savilian Professor of Astronomy, one of two Chairs founded in 1619 by Sir Henry Savile. The interior is an engineering *tour de force* with a 21.5-metre-wide timber roof unsupported by pillars, based on a design by John Wallis, Savilian Professor of Geometry. The exterior is less bold but is enlivened by the surrounding sculptures of emperors' heads, based on Roman boundary posts or 'herms'. To the left is the Clarendon Building (1712–13), the original Oxford University Press, designed by Nicholas Hawksmoor. The turrets in the background belong to the Bodleian Library gatehouse built in 1620 to house the university's muniments and financial deposits. This photograph was taken in 1954.

The Sheldonian and the Clarendon Building have been cleaned, refaced or both. The emperors' heads sculptures are surprisingly still as grubby. A trumpet-playing statue has now appeared on the Clarendon. The Sheldonian is still used for its original purpose. Oxford University Press vacated the Clarendon in 1830 for their new premises on Walton Street, where they are to this day. The Clarendon was used by the university for general administrative purposes until 1975, when it was passed to the Bodleian to provide meeting rooms and office space.

The Old Ashmolean Museum, built in 1679–83, was probably designed by the master mason, Thomas Wood. It is one of the best examples of seventeenth-century architecture in Oxford. By the late nineteenth century the museum's collection, which had become too large to be housed here, was moved to a new building (then called the University Galleries) in Beaumont Street. In this 1950s photograph of the Broad Street entrance, the ravages of time have yet to be reversed. Built in soft Headington freestone, all is being devoured by coal-smoke. The emperors' heads have literally been disfigured.

OLD ASHMOLEAN MUSEUM

Now the Oxford University Museum of the History of Science

Hard Clipsham stone has refaced the wall and pillars supporting the emperors'
heads. The heads themselves, already dirty, have been changed. The one on the
right now sports what looks like aviator's goggles, but are in fact laurel leaves.
The Old Ashmolean, now Oxford University Museum of the History of Science, has
undergone a complete facelift.

NEW COLLEGE LANE FROM THE SHELDONIAN THEATRE

Showing the Clarendon Building, Hertford College and the Bodleian Library

Above: This 1880 photograph is one of the most interesting compositions taken by Oxford-based Henry Taunt. To the left is a very sooty University Printing Press, built in 1712–13 by Nicholas Hawksmoor. To the right, and equally sooty, is the Old Schools Quadrangle of the Bodleian Library, built in 1613. The stonework of these buildings is being devoured by sulphur from coal fires. Directly ahead, New College Lane has to its left a jumble of seemingly eighteenth-century houses. It is more than likely that they are the facades of older buildings. Hidden among them is an octagonal Chapel of Our Lady, built in 1521. These houses had not suffered the effects of smoke pollution to the same extent as their two noble neighbours. Neither has Hertford College (built in 1820–22 by William Garbett), opposite on New College Lane. In the distance is the bell tower of New College's Chapel, built in 1396–97.

Right: Hertford's new student hall of residence, built in 1906, has replaced the jumble of houses on the far left. The doorway to the former Chapel of Our Lady was retained and became the Junior Common Room. The most striking change is the addition of Hertford's famous 'Bridge of Sighs' spanning New College Lane. The former University Printing Press, now the Clarendon Building, has been completely refaced, as has the top floor of the Bodleian. Even Garbett's building at the corner of New College Lane appears sprucer. But the shadows cast by the Bodleian's pinnacles are just as they were in 1880.

THE 'BRIDGE OF SIGHS'

Built by Sir Thomas Jackson in 1913–14

Where is Hertford Bridge, or the 'Bridge of Sighs' as it is commonly known? The second most famous monument in Oxford was not yet built at the time of this 1907 photograph. What is there, to the left, is Hertford College's neo-Jacobean style block of students' rooms, built by Sir Thomas Graham Jackson in 1901–07. To the right is another of Hertford's buildings, erected in 1820–22 by the architect William Garbett for the then Magdalen Hall. The turreted building in the distance is the bell tower of New College's Chapel, built in 1396–97. Halfway down New College Lane, protruding from the block of students' rooms, is some exposed jagged masonry. It is awaiting the arrival of Hertford's new bridge.

Hertford College's bridge (1913–14) was designed by Sir Thomas Jackson in a loosely Renaissance style. It links the college with its block of students' rooms. Why it is commonly called the 'Bridge of Sighs' is anyone's guess, for it bears little resemblance to its venerable Venetian namesake. If anything, it is more like Venice's Rialto Bridge. Although it was tucked away down New College Lane, when it was completed it caused some controversy. Its location enraged several fellows of New College. Hertford was seen as an upstart by New College, which was founded in 1379.

Why should the fellows of New College have to pass under Hertford's fake grandeur to reach their own establishment with its unbroken pedigree, at the end of their own lane? Although once a Hall which could trace its origins back to 1314, Hertford only became recognised as one of Oxford University's colleges in 1740. Later it went into abeyance and had to be re-founded (with Charles Baring's banking fortune) in 1874. Today, the 'Bridge of Sighs' is without doubt Oxford's most-popular backdrop for visitors' photographs.

THE PROSCHOLIUM
OF THE BODLEIAN LIBRARY

One of the oldest libraries in the world

Above: Opened in 1602, the Bodleian is one of the oldest libraries in the world. It is named after its founder Sir Thomas Bodley, a distinguished diplomat and Fellow of Merton College. Since an Act of Parliament in 1911, the Bodleian is entitled to a copy of every book (including this one) published in the UK. It is also entitled, under Irish law, to a copy of every book published in the Republic of Ireland. The Proscholium, loosely translated from Latin as 'in front of the school', formed one of the entrances to the Bodleian that housed part of the Divinity School. Over the doorway is inscribed in Latin: 'Academicians of Oxford! Thomas Bodley has built this library for you and for the Republic of the Learned. May the gift turn out well!' It was built in 1610 to the design of master masons John Akroyd and John Bentley. They were brought all the way from Halifax in Yorkshire because they were more experienced and less expensive than

Oxford masons, who had started a freemasons' guild and were now controlling prices throughout the city. This view was taken in 1958. In the foreground is a statue, designed by Hubert Le Sueur, of a subsequent benefactor, the Earl of Pembroke.

Right: The Proscholium, which has since been cleaned and repaired, became the main entrance to the Bodleian in 1968. The Old Schools Quadrangle has had its paving relaid and the railings surrounding the statue have been reinstated. Akroyd and Bentley's architecture manages to be both formidable and elegant, a difficult act to achieve. The Proscholium's interior is no less impressive; the Bodleian holds literary treasures, including four copies of the *Magna Carta*, Shakespeare's first folio and Shelley's letters.

HERTFORD COLLEGE

The Old Quad, designed by Sir Thomas Jackson in 1890

This is the Old Quadrangle of Hertford College photographed soon after it was remodelled in 1890. Designed largely by Sir Thomas Jackson, its most controversial feature was the French Renaissance–style staircase, a little like the one at the Royal Château de Blois in the Loire Valley. It leads up to Hertford's new hall. This was even more unusual. Jackson located it over his new gatehouse. It is lit on each side by large Venetian-style windows. These can be seen on the upper floor, to the left of the staircase. Jackson's eclectic designs were dubbed 'Anglo-Jackson' by his detractors and nowhere more so than his efforts at Hertford with his staircase and hall, not to mention his 'Bridge of Sighs' over New College Lane.

Jackson's staircase and hall have stood the test of time well. What once raised eyebrows has become one of the most memorable quads in Oxford. The builders' excellent craftsmanship is now complemented by the trees and creepers that soften the original design. Hertford has certainly had a chequered history, starting out as Hart Hall in the thirteenth century, becoming the abortive Hertford College of 1740 and then being re-founded with a large gift of money by the banker Charles Baring in 1874. Yet it and its predecessors can boast some of the most distinguished alumni of the university, including poet and cleric John Donne, Bible translator William Tyndale, political philosopher Thomas Hobbes, satirist and cleric Jonathan Swift and writer Evelyn Waugh.

NEW COLLEGE

Founded by William of Wykeham in 1379

New College was founded in 1379 as St Mary of Winchester College but soon became known as the New College to distinguish it from the older St Mary's (now Oriel) founded in 1324. New College was larger than all the other fourteenth-century colleges combined. It was established as part of a dual foundation by William of Wykeham at the same time as Winchester College, set up to supply New College with its students. These were mostly future clergy, then in short supply because of the Black Death. In this photograph we see New College Lane approaching the fourteenth-century gatehouse. This was the first in Oxford designed as both a tower and as lodgings for the college Warden. From here, the Warden could keep a beady eye on who was coming and going. The niches contain statues of the founder, the angel of the annunciation and St Mary the Virgin. In this photograph, taken in the early 1960s, two students stand by the back wall of the college's cloister. Through the small door in the gate a young woman in a dark coat walks in the Great Quadrangle.

The position of the sun now allows the wall to the right of the gatehouse to be seen more clearly. This was built as a barn to hold food from New College's extensive farmlands, including those at Stanton St John (see page 142). The double yellow lines now lead the eye to the small door in the gate, through which a college gardener trims the edge of the Great Quadrangle's immaculate lawn. Apart from being large, New College's history of academic excellence, substantial endowment, international-class choir and extensive and beautiful grounds make it one of Oxford's most distinguished. Famous alumni include politicians Hugh Gaitskell and Tony Benn, playwright Dennis Potter, Chief Rabbi Jonathan Sacks and actor Hugh Grant.

NEW BODLEIAN LIBRARY

Built in 1937–40 to house the Bodleian's expanding collection

Left: In this early twentieth-century photograph of the junction of Broad Street with Parks Road, two pubs face one another – The Coach and Horses (to the right of H.W. Chaundy) and The King's Arms (right). Both were no doubt popular with students. The roofline of the Coach and Horses, which extends to the shop next door, indicates that they may have once been one building. In any case, its unevenness gives away the fact that both these buildings are older than they first appear. Certainly, the classical facade of the shop is a later addition.

Above: In 1937 the Coach and Horses and its neighbours were demolished. Between then and 1940, the New Bodleian Library was built in their place. Funded by the Rockefeller Foundation, the new building provided more room to house the Bodleian's expanding collection. A tunnel under Broad Street connects old and new libraries. Sixty per cent of the new library's book stacks are subterranean. In this photograph we can see the formal entrance to Giles Gilbert Scott's New Bodleian. Although almost never used (other than for occasional formal ceremonies, for it is inconveniently sited on the corner), those who ever do so are unlikely to know that in the same place they would once have been entering a pub. The shadows cast on the facade of the New Bodleian are from the statues atop the Clarendon Building, behind the camera. The King's Arms is still there with only minor changes to its facade. It is the most popular pub for students to meet in Oxford, a position it has probably enjoyed since the demise of the competition opposite.

HOLYWELL STREET

Owned by Merton College since the thirteenth century

Left: This street was part of Holywell Manor, owned by Merton College since the thirteenth century. It still contains a charming collection of seventeenth- and eighteenth-century houses, as seen in this photograph from the 1970s. An example is Holywell Antiques, which for many years, until 1951, was the home of Knowles and Son, a distinguished Oxford building firm. It was founded in 1797, although it can trace an unbroken history a century before that. The company was responsible, and still is, for much of the building work on Oxford's colleges. The two-storeyed house with three dormers next door is dated 1626 on the brackets to the oriel windows in the timber-framed first floor. Behind the tree, and out of sight as it stands back, is Holywell Music Room where Handel once performed. Reputedly the oldest extant concert hall in the world, it was built in 1748 to the designs of Thomas Camplin, Vice-Principal of St Edmund Hall.

Above: Nothing architecturally has changed since the 'then' photograph. Holywell Antiques is now a printing and copy shop. Holywell Music Room is part administered by the Faculty of Music and by Wadham College, on whose land it stands. It is well used for small-scale events, accommodating up to 250 people. The pavements and the road have been repaved, giving, in the case of the former, a more 'historic' effect. Remains of Oxford's old city wall follow the line of Holywell Street to the south and into New College.

THE UNIVERSITY MUSEUM OF NATURAL HISTORY

Alfred Lord Tennyson described the museum's Gothic style as 'perfectly indecent'

Designed by the Dublin architect Benjamin Woodward, the Museum was built in 1855–60 to take the anatomical and natural history specimens from the Ashmolean Museum as well as provide accommodation for the university's various science departments. Woodward was chosen instead of the eminent E.M. Barry, who had proposed an Italianate building. The poet Alfred Lord Tennyson described Woodward's design as 'perfectly indecent' but it was to mark the beginning of the Gothic style for architecture in Oxford. Woodward brought stone-carvers James and John O'Shea from Ireland to fashion the detail. Following criticisms from the University's Convocation, who had commissioned the building, the stone-carvers retaliated by including caricatures of their critics between the decorative plants, birds and animals. They were instructed to obliterate these insults but some were 'forgotten' and remain. The museum has a bold facade inspired partly by the medieval secular architecture of the Netherlands. To its right, and part of Woodward's design, is the Chemistry Laboratory, modelled, bizarrely to its critics, on the Abbot's Kitchen at Glastonbury Abbey. This photograph was taken in 1915.

Today, although the museum still faces openly onto Parks Road, it is surrounded elsewhere by the university's science buildings. The last one to leave its home in the museum was Entomology in 1978. This photograph was taken from the entrance hall of the Radcliffe Science Library, which is the only place where the same view as the 1915 photograph can be obtained. The library shields Woodward's Chemistry Laboratory building from view. From inside the museum you can reach the adjacent Pitt Rivers Museum, which houses more than 500,000 archaeological and ethnographic objects, including shrunken heads, magic amulets and charms, and an enormous totem pole.

THE UNIVERSITY MUSEUM
OF NATURAL HISTORY

Famous exhibits include the head and foot of a Dodo, extinct for more than 300 years

Above: The interior of Benjamin Woodward's building is a large square court divided into three aisles by iron pillars surrounded by a gallery, from which this photograph was taken in 1870. The ironwork supporting the glass roof was made by Francis Skidmore of Coventry. Around the gallery is an arcade. Its stone columns are each hewn from different British rock. Controversy was not confined to the look of the new museum. Soon after it opened an extraordinary public debate took place under this roof. It was to mark the beginning of our secular age. Samuel Wilberforce, Bishop of Oxford, and Thomas Huxley, Professor of Natural History at the Royal School of Mines discussed Darwin's new theory of evolution. Notoriously, Wilberforce asked Huxley whether it was through his grandfather or his grandmother that he claimed descent from a monkey. Huxley, who was the first to introduce the term 'agnostic' replied that he was not ashamed to have a monkey for his ancestor but he would be ashamed to be connected with a man who used great gifts to obscure the truth.

Right: The only important things that appear to have changed are the exhibits. The extraordinary structure seems to have benefited particularly from the dinosaur skeletons because it resembles a huge skeleton itself. Yet its most famous exhibit is still the head and foot of a Dodo, extinct for more than 300 years. Lewis Carroll featured the Dodo as a character in *Alice's Adventures in Wonderland*, for he and Alice Liddell (the inspiration for his famous protagonist) were frequent visitors here. Although there has been some fading of the decoration of the arches caused by nearly a century and a half of sunlight, the interior of the University Museum looks remarkably fresh. Woodward's building has one of the most compelling interiors in Oxford, perhaps because it manages to look more like it did the day it was opened.

THE NUCLEAR PHYSICS LABORATORY, BANBURY ROAD

Designed by Sir Philip Dowson in 1961

The Nuclear Physics Laboratory (left) was designed by Sir Philip Dowson in 1961 to house a vertical accelerator, with a second accelerator and laboratories at its base. This huge concrete structure fans upwards to provide space for handling the accelerator's components using a 15-ton crane. The side walls, constructed from 18-metre (59-feet) concrete beams, are convex at the base and concave at the top. The enormous size of the two accelerators meant that they and the building which houses them had to be constructed at the same time. In this photograph, taken in the mid-1960s, the overall project is still underway with a conventional high-rise for offices and laboratories being built next to the fan. This high-rise structure was completed in 1969. Next to all this activity, two forlorn Victorian properties await their end.

The Victorian properties have disappeared and in their place is another huge
construction, this time for the Departments of Engineering and Metallurgy. It was
built in 1971–76 and it has Le Corbusier-sanctioned deck access. It cannot be
reached from Banbury Road. The accelerators became defunct in 1997 and the fan
now provides office space for the Astrophysics department with undoubtedly
pleasant views of the city. In 2002 it was renamed the Denys Wilkinson Building, in
honour of the physicist who created Oxford's Department of Nuclear Physics in the
1960s. Dowson has knitted the whole complex together with a massive plinth faced
in bush-hammered concrete. Overall, the structure is relatively free of the water-
stains that this type of building usually attracts.

KEBLE COLLEGE

Butterfield's design made the college an icon of Victorian Gothic Revival architecture

Keble College was founded in 1868 as a memorial to John Keble, a leading light in the Oxford Movement. The Movement was a serious attempt to return the Anglican Church to what was regarded as its catholic, high church roots. A keen supporter of the Movement, William Butterfield was appointed architect. Butterfield decided on a college whose design would be without precedent in Oxford. That and its size would make the college an international icon of the Victorian Gothic Revival. The Pusey Quad, named after one of the Movement's leading intellectuals, was built in the 1870s and photographed here in 1880. As in the rest of the college, the quad is built in brick with elaborate patterns mitigating its almighty proportions. The choice of brick invited levity in the university, to the extent that for some time after its completion, groups of students and dons from many of the university's other colleges made it a regular Saturday afternoon pastime to visit Keble just for a laugh. Keble owns the original version of William Holman Hunt's celebrated work *The Light of the World* (1853–54).

Nothing has been changed to the exterior appearance of Butterfield's grand design. In this colour image, what was once regarded as an absurd decision to use brick in a city where anything prestigious was built of stone, can now be seen to have been inspired. The elaborate patterns of blue and white brick really do make Keble what it is. Even its chimneys get the full treatment. Although every other stone-built college in Oxford has had to be refaced because of the poor quality of the locally quarried material, Keble College can be confidently allowed to remain pretty much as its maker left it. Distinguished alumni of Keble include The Samaritans founder Chad Varah, tenor Peter Pears, *The Independent* newspaper founder Andreas Whittam Smith and Pakistani politician and cricketer Imran Khan.

JESUS COLLEGE

Also known as 'the Welsh College'

Left: On the right-hand side of Turl Street is the facade of Jesus College, refaced in 'Collegiate Gothic' style by J.C. Buckler in 1854–6, only twenty years before this photograph was taken. It is a rather dull effort as well as an anachronistic choice for a college founded by Elizabeth I. Two people stand helpfully outside the gatehouse to give the photographer his scale. On the left-hand side is Exeter College, founded in 1314. It received the same treatment as Jesus a few years before. In the distance can just be seen the tower of All Saints' Church (1701–10) on the High Street. Inset, Jesus students look at messages on the college notice board in 1951. Jesus has always been known as 'the Welsh College', dating back to Hugh Price, a clergyman from Brecon who was the driving force behind its foundation. The college has had a Celtic Library since 1713 and the professorship in Celtic studies is based at Jesus. When this photograph was taken the majority of Jesus' students were Welsh.

Right: Student cycles crowd Turl Street's pavements, whose paving stones have been replaced. Today about 15 per cent of Jesus students are from Wales. The facades of Jesus and Exeter colleges remain unchanged. In the distance, All Saints can be seen clearly. Inset, Jesus College's casually organised notice board has been replaced with a more formal arrangement. In an age of mobile phones and texting, paper messages to individuals are defunct; in their place is the ubiquity of colour-printed posters. Alumni of Jesus include T.E. Lawrence (Lawrence of Arabia), Prime Minister Harold Wilson, television personality Magnus Magnusson and several Archbishops of Wales.

LINCOLN COLLEGE

Founded in the fifteenth century by the Bishop of Lincoln

Lincoln College was founded in Turl Street in the fifteenth century by the Bishop of Lincoln, in whose diocese Oxford then was. Between 1815 and 1819 its frontage, seen here to the left in 1881, was completely refaced by Thomas Knowles. Sulphurous smoke from coal fires and Oxford's gasworks has already despoiled much of Lincoln's stonework. Those elegant gaslights have exacted their price. At the end of the street, repair work is in progress on the tower of All Saints' Church, whose spire is obscured by the large tree. Lincoln College's facade faces Turl Street from Brasenose Lane, to the left, all the way south to the High Street. Turl Street almost certainly took its name from a revolving or twirling gate positioned in the city wall at the street's northern junction with Broad Street. It was demolished in 1722.

Lincoln has been largely re-faced. The gas street lighting has disappeared. A post box has been inserted at the corner with Turl Street and Brasenose Lane. Both streets are now paved in a variety of materials and Victorian-style bollards have popped up, completing the now all-too-familiar visually cluttered look favoured by urban planners when areas are pedestrianised. The end of the large tree means that the impressive spire of All Saints' Church can now be seen at the end of Turl Street. An Oxford landmark, it was built in 1701–10 (the spire was rebuilt in 1718-20) in Italian Renaissance style. The church was declared redundant in 1971 because its congregation had over the years moved away from the city centre. As Lincoln College had been the church's patron since 1475, it was then designated as the college's future library. Distinguished alumni of Lincoln include author and cartoonist Osbert Lancaster, novelist John le Carré, actress Emily Mortimer, Olympic Gold Medallist Stephanie Cook and poet Tom Paulin.

LINCOLN COLLEGE,
FRONT QUAD

'More of the character of a fifteenth-century college than any other in Oxford'

The architectural historian Sir Nikolaus Pevsner said that Lincoln had 'more of the character of a fifteenth-century college than any other in Oxford', to which we could add that its display of modesty and completeness makes it feel homely – a place where you could quite happily live. Here the front quad, photographed in 1962, remains almost the same as when it was first conceived in 1437, although the sash windows are not authentic and the stonework has been given a facelift. Given the absence of water staining, this is most likely a photographic record of completed restoration work.

Since the time of the 'then' photograph, water-staining has made its inevitable
impact on the stonework. Other than that, all is very much the same. Here, a newly
arrived group of freshers are being given a brief history of the college. The college
has been used as a setting for many literary works, including Thomas Hardy's
Jude the Obscure. Lincoln's fifteenth-century buildings have made it a firm favourite
with TV and film production companies. Episodes of *Inspector Morse* and *Lewis* have
been shot here.

LINCOLN COLLEGE, LIBRARY

Designed by Herbert Read in neo-Georgian style

Above: Designed by Herbert Read in neo-Georgian style and built in 1906, Lincoln College's library manages to look grand and bijou at the same time. In this contrast-filled photograph of 1961 it could be a miniature town hall or even a huge doll's house. Its size was not the architect's fault. Room for its construction was restricted in order to avoid sacrificing the garden.

Right: Herbert Read's library was indeed not large enough for the college and in 1975, following its conversion by the architect Robert Potter, Lincoln moved its library to All Saints' Church nearby. In this photograph, thanks to Read's use of robust stone, the re-named Oakeshott Room's facade and detailing, such as the Ionic capitals and the Bishop of Lincoln's mitre atop the coat of arms, remain as crisp today as they did over a century ago.

BRASENOSE LANE

Showing Lincoln, Brasenose and Exeter colleges

Left: Brasenose Lane runs from Turl Street to Radcliffe Square in the distance and in doing so passes three of the most famous colleges in Oxford – Lincoln (immediately to the right, founded 1427), Brasenose (further down to the right, founded 1509) and Exeter (to the left, founded 1314). This photograph of 1890 shows the medieval gutter or kennel running down its centre. Brasenose College, often shortened to BNC, takes its name from the bronze doorknocker (Brazen Nose) once attached to the main gate of Brasenose Hall, the college's medieval forerunner. Brasenose College's distinguished alumni include cricketer Colin Cowdray, writers John Mortimer and William Golding, former Archbishop of Canterbury Robert Runcie, comedian Michael Palin and Conservative Party Leader David Cameron. Exeter College's distinguished alumni include actors Richard Burton and Imogen Stubbs, writers Alan Bennett, Martin Amis and Philip Pullman and the first four-minute miler, Roger Bannister. Inset: through an open doorway, not unlike the one in the main photograph on the right, is a view of the kitchen at Lincoln College in 1953.

Above: The medieval gutter has been retained and the rest of the lane's paving is well preserved. Exeter College's wall, although repaired, has not been refaced and remains in its original condition, as does the lane itself, which is one of the few in central Oxford to escape 'upgrading'. Inset: the original kitchen door has not been used for many years but was kindly opened by Lincoln College's renowned chef, Jim Murden exclusively for this book. Lincoln's kitchen is the oldest in Oxford still operating in the same place. Jim Murden's portrait now hangs in the college's Hall.

CARFAX

Carfax has been the centre of Oxford's shopping and commercial area since medieval times

Left: Carfax is probably where Oxford started. This was where cattle were slaughtered at the junction of four highways running across England, north to south and east to west. Its name is derived from *quadrifurcus*, Latin for four-forked or perhaps *carrefour*, French for crossroads, and itself derived from Latin. From medieval times Carfax has been the centre of the city's shopping and commercial area. The fourteenth-century tower of St Martin's is all that remains of a largely Regency-period church demolished in 1896 to relieve traffic congestion. Its partial replacement, but set back, is the Midland Bank designed by H.T. Hare and built in 1897. Carfax has always been famous, or notorious depending on your point of view, as a busy junction. Yet here the distinguished photographer A.F. Kersting, successfully manages, by using a tripod and very slow shutter speed, to make it appear traffic-free. A billboard reminds the town's youths and its male students of their military obligations under National Service, advising us that this image dates from the 1950s.

Right: The bells of St Martin's still chime and visitors may climb the tower for a splendid panorama of Oxford's skyline. The main change shown in this view of Carfax is the disappearance of the motorists' signposts and the introduction of a pedestrian zone. Through traffic at Carfax was taken away by a convoluted one-way system, the construction of the Oxford bypass and most recently by the M40 motorway. This relieved traffic in Oxford's city centre but was paralleled by an explosion in leisure shopping. This photograph is almost as contrived as the 'then': it was taken in a split second when the view was not obliterated by a continual procession of single-decker buses from competing companies.

CARFAX AND HIGH STREET

'One of the world's great streets. It has everything.' (Nikolaus Pevsner)

Left: In 1907, most of the traffic was still horse-drawn. Tramlines reduced wheel resistance, meaning that horses could pull a much greater weight. Here we see two horse-drawn trams trundling up and down the High Street. As they reached Carfax each driver would switch to the single track. It is possible, given its angle, that this photograph by Henry Taunt was taken over the heads of the horses from the front upper deck of a tram that had stopped for a few seconds to allow him to change the plate. Taunt worked from his studio at 34 High Street between 1885 and 1906. To the left is the spire of All Saints' Church, built to the design of Henry Aldrich in 1701–10 to replace the medieval church whose tower had collapsed.

Above: What is most striking is the similarity of the buildings after over a century. Both left and right, they are practically identical if in better condition, although the attention to conservation is counteracted somewhat by the number of garish shop and road signs. In medieval times the High Street was known as Eastgate Street, as it ran from the East Gate to Carfax. The building to the left is a bank designed in 1900–01 by Stephen Salter.

ST MICHAEL'S CHURCH, CORNMARKET STREET

The tower of St Michael's Church is the oldest remaining building in Oxford

The tower of St Michael's Church is the oldest building in Oxford. It dates from just before the Norman Conquest and once formed part of the northern defence of the town, standing as it did to the side of the long-since demolished North Gate, which gave its name to the street before it became Cornmarket. In the distance is the thirteenth-century tower of St Giles' Church. To the right is a collection of old shops, difficult to date in this 1885 photograph. The architect, designer and writer William Morris married Jane Burden at St Michael's in 1859. At the time of his marriage, Morris was apprenticed to the Gothic Revival architect G.E. Street who had completed a major restoration of St Michael's interior five years earlier. Street's efforts had been strongly opposed by the 'irascible egotist' Reverend Frederick Metcalfe, Vicar of St Michael's between 1849 and 1885.

The rough rag-stone walls of St Michael's remain pretty much untouched after over a century has passed – as they have done for nearly a thousand years. Unlike its younger siblings in Oxford, this tower was built with some of the toughest stone available anywhere in the country. The door of Archbishop of Canterbury Thomas Cranmer's cell can still be seen in the church. It was taken from the Bocardo Prison, which once stood adjacent to St Michael's. It was from the Bocardo that Cranmer was taken on 21 March 1556 to be burned at the stake in Broad Street for his refusal to accept the Roman Catholic faith. The biggest change is to the building next door. It looks as though someone has demolished the building and inserted a medieval replica in its place. There has certainly been a little historic encouragement, but what is seen here are the same timber-framed shops with their later frontages stripped away. What was revealed in 1985–87 was the New Inn, dating back to circa 1386–96, as founded by John Gibbes, Oxford's Mayor and MP. From inside Pret a Manger you can, over a coffee, appreciate a cleverly designed timber frame still in good condition after more than six hundred years.

CORNMARKET STREET

Oxford's main commercial thoroughfare

Left: Cornmarket Street was, and still is, Oxford's main commercial thoroughfare. It was once called North Gate Street after a large gatehouse that stood across the street until 1771, opposite the tower of St Michael's. The tower of the church can be seen in the distance on the right in this 1907 photograph. In the foreground, just seen emerging on the left, is the front of the Clarendon Hotel, once called The Star Inn. Opposite is the Roebuck Hotel, which took its name from the coat of arms of Jesus College. When these were famous coaching inns, a trip to London took six hours and five changes of horses. Down the centre of the road run tramlines. In 1907 trams were still horse-drawn but they were soon to be electrified.

Above: In 1973 pavements were widened, kerbs removed and the street closed to all vehicles except buses, taxis, delivery vans and emergency vehicles. In this respect, it was one of the first pedestrian precincts in the country. In 1999, buses and taxis were excluded. Today it is congested with shoppers, and not just at weekends. The Roebuck was replaced in 1935 by a Woolworths store and subsequently a branch of Boots. The Clarendon was demolished in 1955 and was replaced by yet another Woolworths store, designed in 1956–57 by Lord Holford. His building has a walling of squared rubble with infill panels of slate. Woolworths closed in 1983 and Holford's building became the entrance to the Clarendon Centre shopping mall.

HIGH STREET,
THE COVERED MARKET

Designed by architect John Gwynn in 1773–74

Left: In 1773–74, the architect John Gwynn designed a new market to replace that at Carfax, which had operated since the tenth century. At first it was mainly used by butchers. In this late nineteenth-century photograph, part of Gwynn's classical frontage to the market can be seen, with its High Street entrance to the right. In the Victorian period the market was covered with a glass roof and extended. It then took its present name 'The Covered Market' selling produce such as meat, fish and vegetables, as well as china and other goods. Slatter and Roses's bookshop had been long-established when this photograph was taken. In 1806 Henry Slatter started one of Oxford's early newspapers, the *Oxford University and City Herald*. A four-page weekly costing 6d, it was published at this bookshop from 1833. Above Slatters are rooms used by the Mitre Hotel whose main building is to the right of the market entrance. Next door to Slatters is a china shop, with some of its wares confidently displayed on the pavement.

Above: Gwynne's classical market frontage is in good condition. Slatters has been replaced by two shops; the china shop by just one. Whittard still sells china cups. The Mitre's advertisement has disappeared (it stopped trading as a hotel in the 1960s, see following page), although Gwynne's mock balustrading above the market's entrance now has to compete with an intrusive sign. The Covered Market continues to thrive, selling a variety of quality goods.

HIGH STREET, THE MITRE

Owned by Lincoln College since the fifteenth century

Left: This famous inn on the High Street can be dated back to circa 1300. In the fifteenth century it passed into the ownership of Lincoln College and took its name from a bishop's headdress, in this case the Bishop of Lincoln's, founder of the college. Before the advent of railway travel, The Mitre was one of the greatest of the city's coaching inns. On 28 September 1928 there was a fun attempt to revive the stage coach between Oxford and London when a coach owned by a Captain Mills and a Mr Goddard made the run from the Berkeley Hotel to the Mitre followed by a banquet. This photograph must have been taken a few years later. By then the Mitre had received its AA designation as a recommended destination for motorists. To the left is the entrance to the covered market.

Above: Although the AA sign has disappeared, a rather striking three-dimensional model of a mitre now projects from above the first floor. Yet fundamentally The Mitre appears unchanged, although its ancient and primary function as an inn finished 40 years ago. Since then it has only served as a restaurant. The former hotel accommodation is used by staff of Lincoln College, which, although it's hard to believe, still owns The Mitre after a march of over half a millennium. Today, in addition to the train, there is a low-cost 24-hour coach service to London with the coaches of two companies providing more than 150 journeys a day. Instead of the six hours of the stagecoach, each journey takes approximately 100 minutes. Naturally, the service is very popular with Oxford's students.

HIGH STREET, SOAME'S AND THE RHODES BUILDING

Named after Cecil Rhodes, founder of Rhodesia (now Zimbabwe)

Left: Looking eastwards down the High Street, with The Queen's College (founded 1340) in the distance, this photograph taken in August 1908 concentrates, rather puzzlingly at first glance, on less impressive fare – a commonplace range of buildings of different ages and styles on its opposite side. Our eye is taken to two women pushing prams. The sun highlights the woman in white, attracting our attention to the photographer's shop behind, including the sun-lit advertising on the side. These properties were about to be demolished, making it likely that the photograph was taken by one of Soame's employees as a record for posterity.

Above: Between 1908 and 1911, this heavy-duty neo-Jacobean building was erected for Oriel College (founded 1324) as a new block of undergraduate rooms on the site of Soame's and the other shops. It was designed by Basil Champneys and features, centre-stage, a statue of the person who paid for it: former student of Oriel, Cecil Rhodes. Rhodes was a South African diamond magnate, founder of Rhodesia (now Zimbabwe) and of Oxford's Rhodes Scholarships. Next door is the Old Bank Hotel, formerly a branch of Barclays. Oriel's Rhodes Building would be the last major architectural change to the High Street. The name Soame continues in Gillman and Soame Ltd., official photographers to Oxford University and contractors to many schools and colleges across the UK. Their headquarters are in Bicester, Oxfordshire.

HIGH STREET, ALL SOULS COLLEGE

Built between 1438 and 1442 by Richard Chevynton of Abingdon

Left: This image shows All Souls fifteenth-century facade overlooking the High Street. Richard Chevynton's design was to become the inspiration for many medieval-style college facades, not just in Oxford but nationally and internationally. The house to the right was built in 1704 for the College's Warden, but first occupied by its designer, George Clarke. Beyond the small buildings is the impressive frontage of The Queen's College, designed and built by George Clarke and William Townesend in 1710.

Above: The early morning sun highlights the upper reaches of Chevynton's All Souls facade, drawing attention to the visual importance of the gable ends and the dormer windows as flanking elements for his gatehouse tower. This was the silhouette that was to be much copied. All Souls was founded in 1438 and since the seventeenth century has not admitted undergraduates, only Fellows. A Fellowship of All Souls College Oxford is considered an academic accolade second to none. Sadly, traffic lights for a pedestrian crossing now obscure what was once a grand view of The Queen's College. What was Barclay's (far right) is now the Old Bank Hotel.

ALL SOULS COLLEGE, NORTH QUADRANGLE

Built by Nicholas Hawksmoor in 1716–1720

Above: One of the most astonishing discoveries in Oxford is to wander into the North Quadrangle of All Souls and see for the first time Nicholas Hawksmoor's twin towers, built in 1716–1720. Their lower parts look a little like the western towers of Westminster Abbey, although in fact it is the other way round, for Hawksmoor designed these first. To their left in this 1880s photo is the Codrington Library, also designed by Hawksmoor and paid for from the will of a former Fellow, Christopher Codrington, a rich Barbados sugar planter and slave-owner. The whole extraordinary ensemble Hawksmoor designed in 'Gothic style'. It is actually a classical design throughout with Gothicised adornments. This medieval pretence is dropped inside.

Right: Nothing has changed since 1880. The colours on the 1659 sundial by Christopher Wren (a Fellow of All Souls), which was moved to the North Quadrangle in 1877, can be fully appreciated. What would Wren have thought about his sundial being incorporated into a work by his former pupil? An officer of the College hurries past Hawksmoor's towers, drawing our attention to their surreal cathedral-like scale. Hawksmoor's striking silhouettes were to influence early skyscrapers such as the Woolworth Building in New York City as well as several Soviet-era hotels in Moscow and elsewhere in the former Soviet Union.

HIGH STREET,
ST MARY'S CHURCH

The centre from which the University of Oxford grew

Left: The most prominent building in this long-exposure photograph taken in the mid-1930s is St Mary the Virgin Church. Its magnificent fourteenth-century Decorated Gothic steeple was one of the first dreaming spires to be built in Oxford. From the mid-1200s St Mary's was used for meetings of the university's main governing body, Convocation, and then for degree ceremonies until the Sheldonian Theatre was built in the seventeenth century. St Mary's saw the mid-sixteenth-century show trials of the Protestant clerics, Cranmer, Latimer and Ridley – later commemorated in St Giles' (see page 12). The exterior, notably the tower and spire, was restored in 1856–57 by George Gilbert Scott. In 1892–96 Thomas Jackson undertook more restoration, including work on the pinnacles. Their statues were replaced with new ones by George Frampton. The originals can be seen in the cloister of New College. In the distance is the spire of All Saints. Just behind the large tree to the right is the impressive residence of the Master of All Souls College.

Above: The classic red phone box was doubtless installed as part of the Silver Jubilee of George V. Every stone building in sight has been cleaned and restored and the houses to the right have been re-rendered and decorated. Throughout its history St Mary's has heard many high-profile sermons whose message has been carried nationally. Perhaps the most famous since the last photograph was C.S. Lewis's wartime sermon 'The Weight of Glory' delivered here on 8 June 1942. For those willing to make the climb, there is a magnificent view to be had in all directions from the tower of St Mary's, especially to the south.

HIGH STREET,
THE QUEEN'S COLLEGE

Founded in 1340 and named for Queen Philippa, wife of Edward III

A beautifully lit photograph dating from the early 1920s shows The Queen's College towering over the rest of the street. The college was founded in 1340 and named for Queen Philippa, wife of Edward III. This facade, built in 1730–35, was a redesign by George Clarke and master mason William Townesend, of a proposal by Nicholas Hawksmoor that the college considered impracticable and costly. This frontage is based on the Luxembourg Palace in Paris. Its cupola houses a statue by Henry Cheere of Queen Caroline, who gave £1,000 to the building fund. Since it was erected many visitors have assumed, understandably, that the college was named in her honour, which of course it wasn't. Pevsner called Townesend's masterpiece 'the grandest piece of classical architecture in Oxford'. It was buildings such as those to the left that were often swept aside to make way for a development such as this. Although dwarfed, they have managed to survive.

Alterations to The Queen's College include its cleaned-up appearance, the addition of two flagpoles and the removal of a chimney breast on the roof ridge to the left of the cupola. There are more changes next door. Nearly every shop front and elevation has been completely remodelled, in a studiedly old style. Unpretentious and historically unimportant buildings such as these have only been thought worthy of conservation in the last 30 years or so. The college has always had close links with northern England, especially Yorkshire and Cumbria, and many of its students are from the North. Its Chapel Choir has a reputation as the best mixed-voice choir in Oxford. Distinguished alumni of Queen's include King Henry V, philosopher and founder of University College London Jeremy Bentham, astronomer Edmund Halley, comedian Rowan Atkinson and inventor of the World Wide Web Tim Berners-Lee.

THE QUEEN'S COLLEGE, FRONT QUAD

Based on the Luxembourg Palace in Paris

As with the new facade of the The Queen's College, the Front Quad was inspired by buildings in the style of the Luxembourg Palace in Paris. Here we see a French-style, rusticated open arcade on the ground floor, which stretches round three sides of the quad; the Hall and Chapel being on the fourth side. There were only men's bicycles parked at The Queen's College in 1903. This view shows the south arcade of the quad looking towards the Porter's Lodge. All Oxford colleges have a Porter's Lodge and they can trace their lineage back to medieval religious houses. The Porter's Lodge is the barrier between the parallel worlds of 'town and gown'. The role of the porter is to decide which visitors are to be welcomed and which not, to pass on messages, take deliveries, answer queries and provide intelligence to the head of the college.

Bicycles were barred from the quad many years ago. The Porter's Lodge has been moved to the opposite side and security gates have been installed. Security increased in the mid-1970s when former men-only colleges started to take women students; a time also when IRA bomb threats escalated. Each college has public opening times, which it controls rigorously through its Porter's Lodge. It is interesting to note that this arcade appears to be untouched – a rarity in a city where nearly every exterior stone surface has been replaced since the 1950s. However, on closer inspection (to the right), we can see some subtle improvements.

HIGH STREET, COOPER'S 'OXFORD' MARMALADE

Coffee has been sold from this address since 1650

Left: When this 1905 photograph was taken, 30 years had passed since Sarah Cooper's husband Frank first put her surplus marmalade on sale in his grocery store at 83–84 High Street. During those years Frank Cooper's 'Oxford' Marmalade became so successful that he had to set up his own factory and was exporting Sarah's now famous marmalade around the world, albeit under his own name. Here we see the place where it all started. This was Cooper's main retail outlet, although the early nineteenth-century grand pillars and pilasters were not installed by him. They had a previous existence as the facade of High Street coffee rooms, which were owned by the Angel Inn, and were added to what were originally seventeenth-century buildings with eighteenth-century remodelling. The Angel Inn was demolished in 1876 to make way for the University's Examination Schools, which makes these Regency facades the only trace of its existence.

Above: Frank Cooper stayed here until 1919. These buildings then had a chequered career. They were variously a Twinings branch, a Co-op, a sub-post office and in 1985, Cooper's 'Oxford' Marmalade again. Coopers obtained the lease once more for 84 High Street and sold marmalade as part of a small museum about the company. Sadly, this venture only survived a few years and the next operator was the English Teddy Bear Company. The Grand Café has been the leaseholder of No. 84 since 1997. No. 83 is now a bus drivers' staff room. Throughout their history these buildings have been owned by University College. For the most part, both buildings have been well restored, especially what is now The Grand Café. It is a pity No. 83 suffers a quasi-modernist plate-glass window and doorway. But at least it does acknowledge Sarah and Frank's international success with its plaque, added in 2001. If you are enjoying your *latte* in The Grand Café you may be interested to know that this is where Cooper's 'Oxford' Marmalade was first sold, although it may be more relevant for you to know that you are sipping it on the site of one of the first coffeehouses in Oxford, dating back to 1650.

MAGDALEN BRIDGE AND TOWER

Magdalen's distinguished alumni include Oscar Wilde and John Betjeman

Left: Magdalen College (which retains its fifteenth-century pronunciation 'Maudlen') has a Great Tower that stands sentinel over Magdalen Bridge. These two famous structures have for centuries announced to visitors from London that they have finally arrived at the City of Dreaming Spires. Magdalen Tower was built in 1492–1505. Its design is attributed to master mason, William Rainold. The pinnacled buildings to the right are the southeast corner of Magdalen's Great Quadrangle and were designed and built in 1474–80 by William Orchard. During the Civil War (1642–51) Oxford was a Royalist stronghold and became the headquarters of King Charles I. Magdalen College was a crucial defence post and its tower was used as a vantage point from which to spy approaching enemies. Magdalen Bridge was designed by John Gwynne and was built between 1772 and 1790. Its predecessors reach back to Oxford's beginnings. In this photograph, taken in 1934, we see the egalitarianism of the Oxford bicycle: dons, undergraduates and working men share the road.

Above: The Great Tower of Magdalen College appears to almost shimmer in the early morning sun. Together with the Radcliffe Camera, Tom Tower and the 'Bridge of Sighs', it is an iconic image of Oxford University. At 6 a.m. once a year, as they have done for hundreds of years, Magdalen's celebrated choir sing out their welcome to May Morning from the top of the Great Tower. For years, fuelled with champagne, brave or foolhardy undergraduates added to the festivities by jumping off the bridge into the shallow Cherwell. Magdalen is one of the most visited of Oxford's colleges. This is not surprising given the extraordinary elegance of its buildings, as well as its unique deer park. Distinguished alumni include historian of ancient Rome, Edward Gibbon, playwright Oscar Wilde, poet John Betjeman, actor and comedian Dudley Moore, editor and TV personality Ian Hislop and entrepreneur Martha Lane Fox.

This is the earliest photograph reproduced in this book. It was taken in 1860 and shows the River Cherwell below Magdalen Bridge (1772–90), which can be seen quite clearly in the distance. This bridge and its predecessors is where the great and good were frequently welcomed or took their official departure, as Elizabeth I did on leaving Oxford in 1566. Here the river was fordable and it is quite possible that this is the place from which Oxford took its name. When this photograph was taken it was part of the grounds of Cowley House, built in 1775–93. In the foreground someone has placed two chairs from which to appreciate a charming view. Sitting here it would not be very difficult to imagine Alice's White Rabbit bobbing anxiously past.

MILHAM FORD

Looking towards Magdalen College

Today things have been tidied up to form a still-charming park. A well-manicured sports ground can be seen on the opposite bank. The Cherwell looks as though it has been dredged and channelled. In the summer, punting is popular here – as it has been since circa 1860 when, following the decline of fishing punts, it turned into a popular leisure activity. Cowley House became the nucleus of St Hilda's, which was established as a new college for women in 1893. Its founder was Dorothea Beale, Principal of Cheltenham Ladies College, who established St Hilda's to provide a hall of residence in Oxford for ladies from Cheltenham. She chose the saint of Whitby because Hilda was the first great educator of women in England and as abbess she had 'laid chief stress on peace and love'. In 1958 St Hilda's College acquired these grounds. Distinguished alumni of St Hilda's include feminist author Kate Millet, scientist and academic Susan Greenfield, novelists Barbara Pym and Victoria Hislop, and politician Gillian Shephard.

LOGIC LANE,
UNIVERSITY COLLEGE

William of Durham founded University College in 1249

Left: After centuries of disputed ownership, the medieval Logic Lane was awarded to University College in 1904, three years before this photograph was taken. Its name is supposedly derived from a school of logicians that once existed at its northern end, although an earlier name was Lawdenyslanesine. To the left are the main buildings of University College. To the right are Durham Buildings, designed as halls of residence by the Oxford architect H.W. Moore for University College and completed in 1903. They take their name from William of Durham who founded the college in 1249. Through the arch is the High Street with the dome of The Queen's College peeping above.

Above: The railings have disappeared and the arch is gated, making clear that all we see belongs to University College. The Edwardian Durham Buildings look almost new in their smartness. A contender alongside Balliol and Merton for the title of 'Oldest College in the University', University College is today also one of the largest in its student population; as well as the best-loved in either Oxford or Cambridge, measured by the proportion of former students giving it financial support. Distinguished alumni include poet Percy Bysshe Shelley (who was sent down after writing *The Necessity of Atheism* in 1811 and sending a copy anonymously to the head of every college in the university), Prime Minister Clement Attlee, author C.S. Lewis, *Private Eye* founder Richard Ingram, journalist Paul Foot, physicist and astronomer Stephen Hawking, actor Warren Mitchell, Poet Laureate Andrew Motion and President Bill Clinton and his daughter Chelsea.

65–66 HIGH STREET

Home of Stanford University in Oxford since 1984

These eighteenth-century houses, opposite Magdalen College and owned by them, are more elegant than they may first appear. The first-floor window of No. 65 (left) gives a visual focus to the facade while not competing with the front door and its fanlight. The windows above emphasise the height of the facade by decreasing in scale. These houses are timber-framed and inside is some panelling dating to circa 1730. In this photograph, taken in the late 1970s, this house and its neighbour appear in need of some repair and conservation.

Repair and conservation started in 1984 when Stanford University, Palo Alto, California took from Magdalen College the lease of 65–66 High Street for 52 of their undergraduates. Stanford is one of the leading universities in the United States. It was responsible for Silicon Valley through its graduate students who established companies such as Hewlett Packard, SUN Microsystems (Stanford University Network), Yahoo and Google. For its courses based at 65–66 High Street, Stanford insists on using the traditional and academically rigorous tutorial method perfected over centuries by the University of Oxford. Some of the academic staff also teach in the university.

MERTON COLLEGE, MOB QUAD

Founded by Walter de Merton in 1264

Left: Merton vies with University College and Balliol College as the oldest in the university. It was founded by Walter de Merton in 1264. This is a view of the southwest corner of Mob Quad, built in 1373–78. Taken in 1885, this photograph shows part of the earliest complete Oxford college quad. Merton's Fellows lived downstairs while the upper floors housed the oldest library in Oxford, lit by single-light windows between which the valuable books were chained to stalls. The dormer windows are early seventeenth century and were inserted to provide extra light for the library. Mob Quad, where Fellows and students lived as well as studied, became a blueprint for the college quads of Oxford and Cambridge. Its name has only been used for 200 years or so and was possibly introduced as a humorous description of its occupants.

Above: Although there has been some of the expected re-facing work and repair to door and window frames, the removal of some chimneys and the arrival of a planter, nothing fundamental has changed since 1885. The ancient library is still extant although the ground floor now houses a modern library for students of English, History, Modern Languages, Classics and Philosophy. The lawn is a twentieth-century addition and probably helps muffle echoes in the quad. Distinguished alumni of Merton include poet T.S. Elliot, RAF ace and philanthropist Leonard Cheshire, author Angus Wilson, film critic Derek Malcolm, professors of English J.R.R. Tolkien and John Carey and BBC Director General, Mark Thompson.

ORIEL COLLEGE, FRONT QUAD

Founded by Edward II in 1326

Oriel was founded by Edward II in 1326 and can claim therefore to be the first college in Oxford established by a monarch. It was built on the site of La Oriole, a house owned by the Crown. This house took its name from its 'oratoriolum' or free-hanging upper window and it was this that gave the college its name. This late nineteenth-century photograph shows the Front Quad, which was built in the reign of Charles I. A man stands in front of the porch into which is carved, in honour of that unfortunate monarch, *Regnante Carola* (meaning 'in the reign of Charles'). The college removed the 'papist' centrepiece statue of the Virgin and Child during Oliver Cromwell's puritan tenure as Head of State. They wisely put it back when Charles II was enthroned. To the right can be seen the pinnacles of the tower of Merton College's expansive chapel.

Of all the photographs in this book this must count amongst those where the least has changed, other than the planting. When Princess Elizabeth, Duchess of Edinburgh, visited in 1948 she was greeted by the college's tortoise in this quad. In 1985 Oriel became the last men's college to admit women. Perhaps it is not overly impressed by speed. Distinguished alumni of Oriel include Elizabethan explorer Sir Walter Raleigh, dandy Beau Brummell, churchman and founder of Keble College, John Keble and, fellow leader of the Oxford Movement and eventually Cardinal, John Henry Newman. There are moves in the Roman Catholic Church to seek Cardinal Newman's canonisation. If these are successful, Oriel will have its first saint as an alumnus.

ORIEL COLLEGE, MARY QUAD

Comprising an assortment of buildings ranging from 1639 to 1911

Mary Quad or St Mary's Quadrangle to use its full name, once consisted of a jumble of buildings, as can be seen in this late nineteenth-century photograph. The building to the left was erected as St Mary Hall (1639–40) with a chapel above. To the right the visual linkage of the building to the hall is uncomfortable to say the least. The free-hanging windows, dubbed 'oriel', have always been associated with the college.

The buildings to the right have disappeared and in their place is the Rhodes Building, named after the former Oriel student and founder of Rhodesia (now Zimbabwe), Cecil Rhodes. The Rhodes Building was designed by Basil Champneys and built in 1908–11 as a student hall of residence. In the corner of the quad is Champney's attempt to improve the linkage between two buildings – a somewhat cumbersome, enclosed staircase leading to St Mary Hall, where the chapel is now a library and the hall the Junior Common Room.

CORPUS CHRISTI COLLEGE

Founded in 1517, Corpus Christi is the smallest college in Oxford

Left: Corpus was founded in 1517 and is traditionally the smallest Oxford college with approximately 350 students. The Front Quad, seen in the main photograph from 1979, shows the gate tower that once contained the President's lodgings. The quad's famous sixteenth-century sundial is surmounted by the college's emblem, the pelican. Its selection may relate to the pelican's feeding behaviour, which involves pecking at its fish supper while the blood of the fish runs down its breast. In medieval times, the pelican was thought to be pecking at its own breast to feed its young, which may have led to it being viewed as a symbolic representation of the Blessed Sacrament – the Christian ritual of feeding from the Body of Christ (Corpus Christi). Inset: Thomas Case, President of Corpus Christi from 1904 to 1924 poses with his dog in 1913. Case strongly opposed women being allowed to enter Oxford University although, interestingly, he also strongly opposed Britain entering World War I. He wrote to those Fellows and students thinking of enlisting in 1914 that if they did enrol they would no longer be welcome at Corpus Christi.

Above: Some fairly exotic plants have thrived, protected as they are by the relatively high walls of this small quad. The pelican and its sundial have been gilded, as has the coat of arms over the gatehouse. Inset: Corpus undergraduate Grace Weaver and current President Sir Tim Lankester stand where Case once stood with his dog. A multi-purpose auditorium for the college is being constructed here. Women were first accepted for entry to Corpus in 1979. The ice was broken in 1963 when the college decided that ten ladies should be allowed to dine on two occasions each term in hall, a place where the name of no living woman could be mentioned. Distinguished alumni of Corpus include educator Thomas Arnold, philosopher Isaiah Berlin, poet Al Alvarez, author Vikram Seth, politicians David and Ed Miliband and tenor Ian Bostridge.

CHRIST CHURCH COLLEGE, TOM TOWER

Designed by Christopher Wren and built in 1681–82

This famous gatehouse of Christ Church College, which soars over St Aldate's, is a beautiful architectural mongrel. When in 1529 Henry VIII sacked Cardinal Wolsey, who had founded the college, it stood unfinished until 1681. Then an ambitious Dean of Christ Church, John Fell called in Christopher Wren, architect of St Paul's Cathedral, to finish it as he thought best – and in doing so provide somewhere from which the college could hang Great Tom, a huge bell cast the year before. The central statue is of Wolsey carved in 1719 and erected in 1872. The view through the gate is into Tom Quad, the largest in Oxford. In this 1920s photograph we can see the crucial and masterly transition Wren achieved from the gatehouse's perpendicular lower reaches to his new bell tower. In front of Tom Tower, two porters stand boldly in the sunshine.

Tom Tower's bell tolls 101 times each night to commemorate the number of original scholars plus one at 'The House', as Christ Church is familiarly known. Before Greenwich Mean Time was adopted legally in Britain in 1880, the bell was tolled at 9 p.m. Oxford time. Since then it has been tolled at 9.05 p.m. GMT, reminding those listening that because of the rotation of the earth it is actually 9 p.m. in Oxford whatever GMT adherents may think. In the centre of Tom Quad is a lead copy of Giovanni da Bologna's *Mercury*, placed here in 1928 on a pedestal designed by Edwin Lutyens. In front of Tom Tower, two porters stand discreetly in the shade. Distinguished alumni of Christ Church include founder of Pennsylvania William Penn, preacher Charles Wesley, philosophers John Locke and Alfred Ayer, artist and critic John Ruskin, mathematician and author Charles Dodgson (Lewis Carroll), poet W.H. Auden, physicist Albert Einstein and 13 British Prime Ministers.

CHRIST CHURCH MEADOW
AND 'THE HOUSE'

Christ Church's chapel is also Oxford's cathedral

Above: 'The House', pronounced 'Hice' in older-fashioned Oxford English, is the everyday name within the university for Christ Church. The designation is derived from the general understanding of a church as the House of God, yoked perhaps with the mocking acknowledgement that Fellows and students of Christ Church clearly considered themselves second to none. Christ Church is unique in that its chapel is also Oxford's cathedral. Its choir is very well known and broadcasts frequently. In this view from Christ Church Meadow, taken in 1885, the main silhouette of the college can be seen. Wren's ogee-capped Tom Tower stands to the left of the cathedral spire. In the foreground is part of its meadow, aptly described by Matthew Arnold, Professor of Poetry at Oxford in the mid-nineteenth century, as 'one of the last enchantments of the Middle Ages'.

Right: In the 1950s and 60s there were attempts by the planners to drive a road across the meadow to relieve Oxford's chronic traffic problem. These were finally defeated after a lengthy fight. More manicured than it once was, but with its informality still fiercely maintained, this image shows Christ Church Meadow as a refuge of calm in the heart of Oxford, recalling Matthew Arnold's celebrated lines: 'And that sweet city with her dreaming spires / She needs not June for beauty's heightening'. Unsurprisingly, Christ Church and its meadow has been a popular choice of location for books (*Brideshead Revisited*) and films (*Harry Potter*).

This view, taken in 1875 from Christ Church Meadow, shows Merton's "Fellows' Quad". Built in the early seventeenth century, this was the first major development of a college since the Middle Ages, as well as the first to provide three storeys. From Christ Church Meadow on 4 October 1784, James Sadler was the first Englishman to ascend in a balloon.

CHRIST CHURCH MEADOW
AND MERTON COLLEGE

The site of the first Englishman's ascent in a balloon

The wall, now stripped of ivy, clearly shows the entrance to Fellows' Quad from the meadow. To the left it has been lowered, offering a better view of the meadow from some of the Fellows' rooms. External blinds on the oriel windows have been removed and the pots have disappeared from the chimneys, as presumably they are no longer used. In the foreground the grass is now velvet-smooth, mown with machinery not available in 1875. This does, however, reduce what was an attractive contrast between the pastoral simplicity of the meadow and the ordered symmetry of Fellows' Quad.

ST ALDATE'S

One of the oldest thoroughfares in Oxford

Left: St Aldate's is one of the oldest thoroughfares in Oxford, running as it does north/south from Cornmarket and Carfax to join Abingdon Road at Folly Bridge, which here is behind the photographer. In an earlier age a street such as St Aldate's, photographed here in 1900, was not merely a thoroughfare or a leisure shopping destination. People lived, made things and sold them here. The neighing of horses, the shouting of draymen, the stench of sulphur and horse-dung would all make up life in a street like this. Perhaps it was streets such as St Aldate's with its chaos and clatter, the enemy of academic study, that first prompted the colleges to distance themselves behind their august walls and imposing gatehouses guarded by stern porters.
In this picture Christ Church College's Tom Tower and gatehouse can be seen just down the street. On the opposite side of the street stood a sweet shop where Lewis Carroll's Alice (Liddell), whose father was the Dean of Christ Church, bought her favourite barley sugar.

Above: The main buildings that locate the modern image to the 1900 photograph are Tom Tower (centre), a cream-painted building stretching down on the left and some buildings at the end of the vista. From the position of the gatehouse towers of Christ Church, it is evident that St Aldate's has been widened, probably circa 1926 when the buildings on the right were demolished to make way for the Memorial Gardens. The sweet shop is now called Alice's Shop, selling gifts and trinkets to tourists, as well as providing an additional photo opportunity. You can now turn off St Aldate's into Memorial Gardens, entering in seconds the peace and space of Christ Church Meadow – one of the most pleasant surprises in Oxford.

FOLLY BRIDGE

The first bridge to be built over the Thames near Oxford

Left: Folly Bridge took Oxford's main north/south axis across the Thames via St Aldate's and Abingdon Road. It was the first bridge to be built over the Thames near the 'oxen ford' and this version dates from 1825–27. In this lively scene from 1900 we see the launching of a lifeboat from Salter's Boatyard. The warehouse to the right was built in 1781. Salter's also made The Oxford folding lifeboat – visible in the yard to the rear – four of which were carried on the *Titanic*, which sank in 1912.

Above: The bridge now carries traffic via Abingdon Road and the suburb of New Hinksey to the Oxford Bypass. The Georgian warehouse is now The Head of The River pub with the yard becoming a popular place in warm weather for a drink and something to eat. A boat-crane has been retained for added character. The pub was named in the 1970s from the description of a rowing race held as a procession against the clock. Punts may be hired at Folly Bridge.

VIEW TOWARDS FOLLY BRIDGE

Where Christ Church Meadow runs down to the Thames

Above: This photograph was taken in 1900, from a pontoon used to board punts and other river craft. With heavy equipment and a slow shutter speed, the photographer would certainly have had to ensure a placid river before exposing the plate. The buildings to the left are boating yards. These are still owned by Salter's Boatyard, from which punts may be hired. Although the river there is crowded with boats, it still evokes a peaceful scene.

Right: There is no longer a pontoon so this photograph is taken from a slightly different position on the riverbank. Fortuitously, this gives a better view of the buildings to the left, which have been spruced up. Behind the white-painted building can now be seen an idiosyncratic flint house built for Joseph Caudwell, an accountant, in 1849. A post-modernist building for Hertford College and a new footbridge have joined the grouping. Landing stages and boats are still moored here as they were over a century ago. Here Christ Church Meadow runs down to the Thames ensuring that this part of Oxford remains popular for walks throughout the year.

THE MORRIS GARAGE,
ST ALDATE'S

A city-centre showroom for Oxford's famous Morris cars

This showroom for Morris cars was built in 1932. In 1975, when this photograph was taken, the once-celebrated Oxford manufacturer of reliable, sensibly priced cars for the growing middle classes had long been subsumed into the British Motor Corporation – later British Leyland, with disastrous results. The Princess cars standing here were some of the last models to carry the Austin and more upmarket Wolseley badges. Morris Garages also gave its name to the well-known marque MG, which is still manufactured, albeit in Shanghai.

The former front door for Morris Cars is now Oxford's courthouse. Although the
doors and windows have been changed, these blend successfully with the early
1930s architecture, to the extent that no one would know unless it was pointed
out. The characteristic bronze lamps, inspired by antique torches, remain in place.
Where you may once have bought a car, you may now appear for a driving offence.

THE MORRIS FACTORY

By the early 1970s, 20,000 people were employed at Morris Motors

William Morris started his company in 1910 at the corner of Longwall Street and Holywell Street but by 1913, with the success of his 'Bullnose Morris', he needed to move to these larger premises at Hollow Way, Cowley. The factory buildings were originally Hurst's Grammar School, a public school for 'middle-class boys' where Morris's father had been educated. The site became a military college and, when Morris bought it, it was a vacant engineering factory. In this photograph from 1913 a sign painted across the facade of the former school reminds visitors unequivocally of its new purpose. To the right, what looks like a new shed has been erected. This 'shed' was the beginnings of a factory that was to become the largest manufacturer of cars in Britain.

Despite some unsympathetic renovation work, the former school and car factory is
in remarkably good condition today. This is now a private housing development and
no trace can be found of Morris Motors – not even an external plaque to honour its
illustrious past. By the early 1970s, 20,000 people were employed at the Morris
works, which by then included Pressed Steel Fisher. The factory was just behind
where this photograph was taken and is now the Oxford Business Park. In 2001
BMW took over what was by then called the Rover Group and now manufactures the
Mini on the opposite side of the Oxford Ring Road. Although nowhere near the size it
once was, this car factory is still the largest industrial employer in Oxfordshire. The
Morris name lives on in the Oxford Bus Museum in Witney, which includes the
Morris Motors Museum.

Oxford's prison was begun on the site of the castle gaol in 1785. In this 1883 photograph, the gatehouse can be seen flanked by the prison's outer walls. Surmounting the tower to the right of the gatehouse is a platform. Until 1863 this was used for public executions and although defunct for 20 years, it was there as a stern reminder of a society that supported capital punishment.

OXFORD CASTLE PRISON

Built on the site of the castle gaol in 1785

In 1969 the prison's 1850–52 cell block was used as a film set for *The Italian Job*. Subsequently it has featured in TV's *Porridge* and *Bad Girls*. It closed as a prison in 1996 and was then converted, as part of a development including shops and restaurants, into a hotel. The hotel is a member of the aptly named Malmaison group and is the only prison turned into a hotel in the country. Good modern hotels always aim to provide a measure of luxury escapism for their guests. This one does it very well, with an added dose of vicarious irony.

REWLEY ROAD RAILWAY STATION

Now the Said Business School

Left: On a site previously occupied by the thirteenth-century Rewley Abbey, Oxford's first railway station was designed and built in 1851 by Fox, Henderson and Company, who were then building the Crystal Palace for the Great Exhibition in London. Here carriages await train passengers beneath the elegant entrance arcade. This charming scene was recorded just before the outbreak of World War I, when it was part of the North Western Railway line. A century after it was opened, Rewley Road was closed to passengers but was in use as a goods yard until 1984, after which it remained unused.

Above: The replacement of Rewley Road Station with the Said Business School provoked controversy from the beginning. The business school was established with a £23 million gift from Syrian/Saudi arms dealer, Wafic Said. Several sites were considered and finally the station was agreed on. There was no public enquiry and it became occupied by protestors. A long and expensive eviction order eventually removed them. The Said Business School opened on Bonfire Night 2001 to a clamorous student demonstration. It was seen as a shameless reminder of a huge and controversial arms contract between the UK and Saudi Arabia, brokered by Said. In 2003, Mr Said received the new Sheldon Medal, established by Oxford University to honour those offering exceptional support. The green projection on top of the building, designed by architects Edward Jones and Jeremy Dixon, is considered one of the most modern of the dreaming spires.

OXFORD UNIVERSITY PRESS, WALTON STREET

The largest university press in the world

Oxford University Press traces its origins back to the late fifteenth century. It moved from the Clarendon Building in Broad Street to Walton Street in 1830. The OUP first made its fortune on the production of bibles and the *Oxford English Dictionary*. These were exported in the Victorian period and early twentieth century throughout the British Empire and the United States. In this photograph from 1953 an employee stands alongside the children's books delivery van, parked just inside the main entrance of the OUP. This part of the east front was built in Roman style in 1826–27 by architect Daniel Robertson.

Although there has been some wear, tear and repair, Robertson's austere Roman-inspired architecture has an eerily timeless quality, emphasised here in its detailed proportion and restraint. Today the OUP is the largest university press in the world. In 2000, its famous dictionary was launched online. Inevitably, it no longer has a children's van. The inset photograph shows the Old Quad, with the arched entrance from the main photograph visible far right.

THE DYSON PERRINS LABORATORIES AND LECTURE ROOM

Designed by Basil Ward and built in 1957–59

Left: Dyson Perrins, of the celebrated Lee & Perrins Worcestershire Sauce company, was a generous benefactor, especially to educational institutions. He funded the building of this laboratory in 1957–59 to further research in organic chemistry. Organic chemistry had first been established here, in what is known as the Science Area, in 1916. Sadly, Perrins died in 1958 and did not live to see the new laboratories completed. The university honoured Mr Perrins by naming the building after him. The architect was Basil Ward of Ramsey, Murray, White and Ward. This daring building photographed in 1960 provides a focus for those surrounding it. This, rather like the library designed for Lincoln College by Herbert Read half a century before, could, in its self-contained perfection, almost be a doll's house – in this case designed and built by a modernist architect for their child. When it was completed it was described by the Oxford Design Society as 'an exciting display of structural virtuosity'.

Above: The study of organic chemistry has moved to the Chemistry Research Laboratory on South Parks Road and the Perrins building is now used by Oxford University Geography Department. Gone is the dramatic underside supported on two tapered pillars. This sleek design has been cancelled out by a non-descript fill-in. The impressive silhouette of Ward's original building has also been spoilt by a clumsy metal balustrade that runs along the length of the roof. Despite these additions, which discredit Basil Ward's design, Dyson Perrins Laboratory can boast two Nobel Prize in Chemistry winners – Lord Todd and Sir John W. Cornforth, who both worked here in their early careers.

HEADINGTON HILL HALL

Rebuilt by James Morrell as a neo-Italianate mansion in 1856–58

In the nineteenth century vast fortunes were made by brewers who assiduously sought stately piles and titles to match. Yet in Victorian England snobbery was not to be bypassed with ease. Once in the House of Lords a new peerage was usually mocked behind the recipient's back as a beerage. James Morrell of Morrell's Brewery, wise enough to avoid that indignity, was quite content between 1856 and 1858 to rebuild the family house, Headington Hill Hall, originally built in 1824, to the east of Oxford. His neo-Italianate pile, although hardly a grand Tuscan villa, is nevertheless quite splendid. It stood at the top of the hill, hence its name, and although on the outskirts of Oxford it was surrounded by 3,000 acres in which James planted some rather exotic trees. In 1878 Oscar Wilde attended a fancy dress May Day Ball here. In the early twentieth century Lady Ottoline Morrell owned the hall and for a time it became a retreat for the Bloomsbury Group. Here it is as it appeared in 1900.

In the second half of the twentieth century Headington Hill Hall became the headquarters and home of the discredited entrepreneur, Pergamon Press publisher and *Daily Mirror* owner, Robert Maxwell. He leased it from Oxford City Council, describing it as the 'best council house in the country'. It is now the headquarters of a more respectable organisation, Oxford Brookes University, which started life in 1865 as the Oxford School of Art. Brookes, as it is called in Oxford, is one of the leading new universities in the UK. It has 19,000 students and has a reputation for the quality of its teaching and research, especially in architecture, art, economics, computer science, motor-sports engineering, history, modern languages and publishing.

STANTON ST JOHN

Stanton St John's most famous son is John White, promoter of Massachusetts

Left: The stone-built villages near Oxford were as English in appearance as it was possible to be. Stanton St John, which is east of Oxford and photographed here around the time of World War I, was no exception. For centuries much of its land and property was owned by New College Oxford. They still own some of it. John Milton's grandparents are buried in the churchyard. Its most famous son, however, is John White (1575–1648), Fellow of New College between 1600 and 1606 and promoter of a new Puritan colony for the New World: Massachusetts. Judging by the sign over the front door, the cottage on the left was a village shop or possibly a pub, although traditionally pub signs were displayed at right angles to the building to attract the attention of thirsty travellers unfamiliar with their surroundings.

Above: One of the advantages of having an Oxford college own a property was the disregard they held for fashionable modernisation schemes, although many of their tenants would no doubt have seen it differently. It therefore became an attractive opportunity when an 'unspoilt property' owned by an Oxford college for centuries was put on the market. In Stanton St John this has happened increasingly in the last 30 years or so, as it has in other villages around Oxford. From the 1970s onwards, a home such as this became, for a growing number of Oxford house-hunters, a dream come true.